Learning in Contemporary Culture

Learning in Contemporary Culture

Series Editor: John Sharp

Will Curtis and Alice Pettigrew

LearningMatters

First published in 2009 by Learning Matters Ltd

British Library Cataloguing in Publication Data
A CIP record for this book is available from the British Library.

ISBN: 978 1 84445 200 2

Cover design by Topics – The Creative Partnership
Text design by Code 5
Project Management by Swales & Willis Ltd, Exeter, Devon
Typeset by Kelly Gray
Printed and bound in Great Britain by TJ International Ltd, Padstow, Cornwall

Learning Matters Ltd
33 Southernhay East
Exeter EX1 1NX
Tel: 01392 215560
info@learningmatters.co.uk
www.learningmatters.co.uk

FSC
Mixed Sources
Product group from well-managed
forests and other controlled sources
Cert no. SGS-COC-2482
www.fsc.org
© 1996 Forest Stewardship Council

Contents

The authors

Dr Will Curtis is Education Subject Leader and Senior Lecturer in Education Studies at De Montfort University. He leads modules in Philosophy of Education, Learners and Learning, and Radical Educations, and he supervises students at undergraduate and postgraduate levels. He has 12 years' experience of teaching on a wide range of programmes in further and higher education and has a longstanding research interest in the relationship between learning and culture. Will is currently on the Executive Committee of the British Education Studies Association.

Dr Alice Pettigrew is a researcher currently based at the Institute of Education, University of London. Recently she has worked as a visiting lecturer at the University of the West of England, where she taught undergraduate courses in Education and Social Justice with a particular focus on gender theory and sexuality, as well as ethnicity, race and multicultural citizenship. Her research has examined the relationships between education and identity from a variety of social scientific perspectives.

Acknowledgements

The authors and publisher would like to thank the following for permission to reproduce copyright material: Trentham Books Ltd (**www.trentham-books.co.uk**).

Every effort has been made to trace the copyright holders and to obtain their permission for the use of copyright material. The publisher and authors will gladly receive any information enabling them to rectify any error or omission in subsequent editions.

Introduction

It is a central contention of this book that learning is, and always has been, a cultural activity. What, where, how and why we learn are each influenced by the cultural contexts in which all learning encounters take place.

Our book recognises that 'culture' itself is a slippery and contested concept. Often when the word is used, it seems to imply that 'cultures' are discretely bounded individual entities: that there is a patchwork quilt of different 'ways of life' that could be mapped to coincide with territories – nations, regions and/or cities – in geographical space. We think that this understanding is problematic. 'Culture' – in terms of shared norms, values, languages, tastes or beliefs – can operate on a variety of different, sometimes overlapping, sometimes contradicting scales.

The boundaries between one culture and another are seldom very clear. Throughout this book, the framework of the British nation is often identified or implied; however, it could be argued that many of the phenomena discussed here are characteristic of wider trends across Europe for example, or common to many 'Western' societies, if not extending right across the globe. Others might in fact relate primarily to specific regions within the British nation, or only to urban areas, or to particular communities within the population as a whole.

It is equally problematic to conceive of cultures as fixed and static over time. For culture is not only active and dynamic but impacted upon by wider social, economic and political change. We suggest that in recent years such change has been particularly dramatic, and contemporary culture offers challenges to and opportunities for learning that are altogether new. When we talk of 'contemporary culture', on one level we are referring very simply to the period we are currently living through. However, we also want to argue that in some respects, recent decades represent a significant break from the past. Important recent change includes:

- rapid and increasing technological innovation;
- dramatic and extensive economic and industrial restructuring;
- changes to the structure of both the labour market and 'traditional' family relations;
- the movement of people, goods and ideas further and faster than ever before;
- the ascendancy of an economic and political system known as neoliberal capitalism;
- a loss of confidence in both moral and scientific certainties following twentieth-century atrocities such as the use of the atom bomb and the Nazi death camps of the Holocaust.

We do not want to present an ahistorical perspective and are interested in the relationships – continuities and disjunctures – between the present period and the past. In particular, we recognise the importance of historical periods known as 'the Enlightenment' and later 'modernity'. These played a crucial role in framing dominant contemporary perspectives on what learning is, what learning is for, and how, when and where learning should take place. We argue that it was a consequence of modernity that 'learning' became narrowly conceived as something that only formal schools and trained teachers can or should facilitate. We believe that in contemporary culture, a broader conception of learning is not only possible but necessary, and are concerned to ask, what kind of learning and learners does the twenty-first century require?

The structure of the book

There are a number of central themes that run throughout the book. In some sense, these are the learning outcomes of the book as a whole. After reading it, you should be able to:

- uncover distinctive characteristics of contemporary culture;
- recognise that a culture characterised by freedom, complexity and fluidity contains enduring power inequalities;
- outline and assess the opportunities and threats to learning that result from these characteristics;
- make sense of learning as a cultural activity;
- understand the relationship between culture, learning , community and nation;
- identify the forms of learning encounters that are most appropriate within contemporary culture.

Chapter one sets the scene by unpacking some familiar understandings of the concept of culture, and describes the ways in which learning is best characterised as a cultural activity. It attempts to identify key features of contemporary (British) culture and draws attention to the opportunities and obstacles these present for learning in the present day.

Chapters two to six make use of five different disciplinary perspectives on education. Chapter two offers an historical overview examining the role of learning and innovation in creating cultural communities and instigating cultural change. It demonstrates how Enlightenment thinking, industrialisation and the advent of the modern nation-state gave rise to centrally controlled, institutionalised systems of education: how scientific enquiry, rationality and progress became the driving forces of change; how teaching was professionalised; and how learning became an activity restricted to formalised times, places and activities.

Making use of a philosophical perspective, the third chapter explores how these values and strategies fit within contemporary culture. The certainty and homogeneity of modernity are, to some extent, replaced by complexity, fragmentation and doubt. Three Enlightenment ideals – universal knowledge, objective morality and legitimate authority – are examined within the cultural settings of the present day. All three are now open to contestation, resulting in both new sources of conflict and new possibilities.

Chapter four approaches these contemporary concerns from a psychological perspective. In recent years a number of influential psychologists have acknowledged that learning is a social and cultural activity. Their theorisations demonstrate how the cultural context in which learning takes place has a considerable bearing on the experiences of the learner. Drawing on social constructivist and 'learning to learn' literature, the chapter asks what types of educational experiences and activities are most effective in preparing young people for the complexity and unpredictability typical of contemporary culture.

Relationships between national government and formal systems of learning are examined in Chapter five. Using examples drawn from three recent policy initiatives, the chapter identifies competing governmental agendas for education and discusses the competing cultures of learning that policy can help to create. It suggests that, in line with contemporary culture in general, recent policy direction in Britain is beset with contradiction and simultaneously offers both obstacles and opportunities.

The focus of Chapter six is the 'micro-level' interactions that take place between staff and students in schools. It is framed by theoretical understandings drawn from sociology and emphasises the role of schools in (re)producing differences between students, exploring the relationships between formal education and persistent social inequalities. With reference to gender, race and ethnicity and socio-economic class, it reminds us that official classroom cultures are not the only set of expectations that young people have to negotiate in constructing their (learner) identities.

Chapter seven takes a slightly different approach to the previous chapters in examining how the concept of culture itself has been used and understood in British educational practice and policy. It builds on arguments developed throughout the book and asks what forms of knowledge – and of learning – are needed to equip students for contemporary *multi*cultural citizenship.

The final chapter looks to alternative sites of learning. Using the critiques of formal schooling originating from the 'unschoolers' and 'deschoolers', it indicates that radically different cultures of learning exist in society today. It shows how the philosophies of Neill and Freire and the approaches to schooling of Steiner and Montessori provide a more human-centred perspective on learning, in contrast to formal schooling. It recognises that there are overlaps between these cultures of learning, especially in a climate where community relations and e-learning are increasingly mainstream preoccupations. The chapter concludes by reflecting on the lessons formal education might take from these alternatives.

There are practical, critical thinking and reflective task boxes within the book. Figure icons within the boxes indicate whether the task is designed as a group project or a task to be worked through on your own.

Reflective Task

Thinking about how culture shapes your own learning identity

Read about the following 'characters of studentship'. They are taken from an ethnographic study of A level students (Curtis, 2008) but you should find them useful in considering your own higher education learning identity. They are the cultural sites that shape learning – both facilitating and limiting it. They will help you to think about how your own learning identity is influenced by the classroom cultures you participate in.

- *Pilgrimage*: the pilgrim views their education as a journey toward specified goals. While those goals are increasingly likely to change, the pilgrim wants to feel that they have direction, that they are moving forward. They ask questions like, 'How will this help me reach my goals?'.
- *Romanticism*: for the romantic, learning is associated with personal development. They want to feel that they are being given opportunities to grow and to be challenged and stimulated. Motivated by a 'love of learning', they seek the rich and deep learning experiences that are currently inhibited by content- and assessment-heavy curriculum. They ask, 'Can I go and explore this on my own?'.
- *Tourism*: the tourist continuously seeks new and different learning experiences, needing to keep moving and 'travel light'. Schooling is a passing visit for them, where they want the freedom to try new things, to engage with new ideas and to meet new people. They ask, 'Is this new and exciting?'. Permanence and constraint are to be avoided.
- *Consumerism*: consumers want to 'shop around' and get the best service they can. They are concerned with high standards and with the quality of the learning opportunities they are being provided with. They ask, 'What am I getting from this?'. If they are not satisfied with the answer, they will complain or leave.

- *Reactionism*: the reactionary seeks certainty, especially when things seem uncertain. They dislike or fear innovation, risk, or alternative learning and teaching strategies. They ask teachers questions like, 'How do I write this in an exam?' or 'Why don't you just tell us the right answer?'.
- *Estrangement*: the stranger is detached and distant. They are not engaged with learning, are reluctant or unwilling to participate in group activities and want to be somewhere else. They ask questions like, 'Why am I here? Why am I so different from everyone else?' and 'What is the point of this?'.

Consider the extent to which your own learning identity is shaped by these characters of studentship.

- Which characters are you most/least aware of in your own learning identity?
- Do some impact on you more in some learning settings (depending on contexts such as the teacher, the group, classroom spaces, days and times of the week, tasks and activities)?
- What situations make you ask the types of questions that are typical of each character?
- Why do you think that is?
- Are you aware of other characters that are shaping your learning identity?

Chapter 1

Culture and learning

Learning outcomes

By the end of this chapter you should be able to:

- demonstrate that culture is a complicated concept with a variety of contested meanings and uses;
- distinguish between a number of features commonly used to identify and examine culture as a shared way of life, including beliefs, norms, tastes, values, roles, language and artefacts;
- recognise that learning is a cultural activity;
- understand some of the ways in which contemporary culture might offer both challenges to and opportunities for contemporary constructions of learning.

Chapter outline

'Culture' appears a very familiar term and yet it has been described by writer Raymond Williams as *one of the two or three most complicated words in the English language* (1983, page 87). This chapter examines where some of this complication lies, and outlines a number of possible interpretations and uses for the word. It builds upon the seemingly straightforward definition of culture as a 'way of life' with identifying markers such as beliefs, norms, tastes, values, roles, language and artefacts. Most significantly, culture should be understood in active rather than passive terms, as it takes a certain degree of action and intention to produce and reproduce meanings, understandings and expectations that are shared. From this perspective, the chapter asks, what shared meanings and collective understandings can be identified within Britain today? Where are they being made? Why? And by whom? Given the fluidity, speed of change and plurality of influences upon contemporary life, does it continue to make sense to talk about a single, shared, dominant culture at all?

The chapter outlines relationships between culture and learning and argues that how, where, what and why we learn can all be shaped, enabled and/or constrained by the cultural expectations that dominate. It also suggests that the distinctive characteristics of contemporary culture offer both opportunities and threats to learning.

Culture as a contested concept

Learning is a cultural activity. Learning encounters do not take place in a vacuum: teachers train to teach, students are enrolled in school, policy makers and professional experts design curricula and course materials. In each case, these encounters are influenced by wider shared expectations – of how a teacher should behave, of who should be at school and when, and of what sort of information a Year 9 history textbook should contain. Such expectations do not appear from nowhere, nor are they constant or consistent in different parts of the world or over time. In fact, they are closely related to the cultural contexts in which all learning takes place. But what exactly does 'cultural context' mean here? And what specifically is implied by describing learning as a 'cultural' activity?

Reflective Task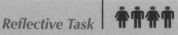

Look at the following statements and consider the way that culture is being presented and understood. In each case, compile a list of characteristics, objects, or concepts that culture may be referring to. Can you think of any alternative words that could have been used? Do the replacement words make sense if used in all of the remaining statements? If not, why not? Can you think of any other examples of how the word 'culture' could be used?

Try to come up with your own dictionary-style definition for the term. Do the examples below help or hinder your task?

* *Among his colleagues at the university, Paul often felt uncultured by comparison.*
* *I don't like the way they treat girls and women, but I guess it's just to do with their culture.*
* *Come to our traditional Native American reserve for an authentic cultural experience.*
* *Police Chief attacks 'Asbo Culture' as crime rates soar.*
* *Increased funding required for the Department for Culture, Media and Sport.*
* *Multicultural policy is failing our inner cities.*
* *Staffroom culture of silence to blame for increased bullying in schools.*

One of the reasons the word 'culture' is so complicated is that it is regularly used in a number of very different ways. Robert Bocock (1992) provides a useful history of the word.

Culture and 'cultivation': distinguishing 'high' from 'low'

Bocock tells us that when it was first introduced to the English language, 'culture' referred to the cultivation of land to grow crops and rear livestock: think of the word 'agri*culture*' as it is used today. This meaning is no longer very common but its history is significant: here culture referred to a process of 'taming' and 'domesticating', turning unruly vegetation and wild animals into manageable farmland, cattle and pets. By the seventeenth and eighteenth centuries, this understanding had been extended to human beings. 'Cultivation' was now seen as something that could be applied to the human mind. 'Culture' began to reflect 'refinement' and 'civility'.

However, eighteenth-century social commentators did not seem to think that *all* human minds could be 'cultivated' in the same way. Some minds were seen as more 'refined' than others; some tastes, activities and behaviours more 'cultured'. Existing relationships of economic and political power were mapped onto and reflected through understandings of culture and cultural value here: it was the aristocratic elite who were first able to define what being 'cultural' meant. They did so narrowly in terms of those forms of artistic expression and intellectual scholarship that reflected their own interests and expertise. The lifestyles, loves and labours of the common man and woman were derided as 'uncultured' by comparison. In many respects, these distinctions endure today.

Some critics might argue that for something to be culturally worthwhile – to count as what might be termed 'high' culture – it must be difficult, not immediately easy to engage with, exclusive. More accessible things with wider appeal are designated 'low' or 'popular' culture and scarcely awarded the same significance or respect. And there is an important educational implication of this. One of the roles of a national education system might be considered the transmission of knowledge about and appreciation of a people's shared cultural heritage. But whose cultural output should be celebrated? Which paintings immortalised in art history textbooks and which novels included in course requirement reading lists? Is culture what you find in art galleries, theatres and opera houses – or is it found on street corners, in graffiti art, soap operas or gossip magazines?

Culture as a 'distinct way of life'

Perhaps the most familiar understanding and use of culture that Bocock describes is the whole 'way of life' of a particular group. Sometimes culture is used to refer to behaviours shared by all of humankind, but when used by anthropologists and other social scientists, it more commonly focuses on differences between identifiable groups. This broad definition could include all intellectual, emotional and behavioural characteristics transmitted through social interaction. Of particular interest are *shared* understandings and ways of making sense of the world. When studying a culture from this perspective, a social scientist would traditionally look to identify a number of characteristic features.

Norms are the expectations for 'normal' behaviour. These might be formalised through law: in Britain for example, you can only be legally married to one person at a time. They might also be informal: although not spelled out anywhere, it is a norm today for people to have a series of faithful partners, known as 'serial monogamy'.

Values are the underlying principles that norms are based upon: the ideals or morals that provide the foundation for society. Modern Western cultures tend to emphasise values such as individualism, secularism, justice, equality, freedom and democracy. The monogamous norms identified above are underpinned by values like faithfulness, loyalty and trust. The recent introduction of the 'serial' dimension of monogamy largely comes from the increasing significance of freedom as a core value of contemporary Western life. Again, a culture's values may be made explicit, as in the French motto *Liberté, Egalité, Fraternité*, or hidden from conscious view.

Beliefs are the propositions collectively held to be true. They might be concerned with knowledge (statements of fact) or with morality (statements of value). They are held to varying degrees.

* Absolute beliefs are the statements that we *know* are true: for example, that there are 31 days in January. The veracity of these claims is taken for granted. We do not question their accuracy: they are certain and we will refer to them as 'knowledge'.
* Strong beliefs are the claims we are convinced by, but that are open to contest. While we are likely to be very attached to our strong beliefs, we can at least acknowledge that alternatives do exist.
* Weak beliefs are the claims that we are attracted to, but that we are not entirely married to. These are beliefs that are open to persuasion and can be abandoned without too much discomfort. For example, an individual might believe that nuclear power is dirty and dangerous, but be convinced otherwise by new scientific evidence, technological advances or economic necessity. However, for an environmental activist, an opposition to nuclear power may be one of their strongest beliefs.

It is worth noting here that even the most absolute beliefs are in fact culturally framed. The knowledge that there are 31 days in January derives from the Gregorian calendar, but this too is culturally specific. The Mayans of Central America for example, had a completely different way of conceiving the passage of time.

Roles are the norms that are attached to the particular positions we occupy within a society, a family, a workplace or any other social grouping. Like norms, our roles can be formal (defined by rules or laws) or informal (shaped by convention, expectation or social desirability). An example of the former is that a doctor will write appropriate medical prescriptions for her patient and an example of the latter is that she will not write these prescriptions while wearing hot pants and listening to Kylie Minogue.

Tastes are the things we like and do not like, from foods, to music, to other people. While these appear highly personal, they are also enabled and constrained by culture. Prevailing tastes of a culture shift over time. In the seventeenth century, for example, people gathered together to enjoy the punishment of criminals in very public and brutal spectacles (Foucault, 1991). Organs spilled out to the delight of the crowds. Contemporary culture seems generally repulsed by the less 'civilised' aspects of humanity (see Norbert Elias' *The Civilizing Process* for an early account of this). Today, prisoners serve out their punishments behind giant walls, hidden from the gaze of the public. In fact, the 'distasteful' aspects of human life (including pain, punishment, death, medical treatment) are hidden from public view.

Perhaps more than any of these other features, tastes illustrate a key characteristic of culture (and one we shall be referring to throughout the book). Tastes vary widely *within* culture. Consider the tastes chosen in opposition to the mainstream as part of defining who we are as an individual. In a contemporary culture that celebrates difference, propagating alternative tastes is one of the most visible ways of standing out. Taking the above example, while the mainstream might show revulsion to torture, a significant minority openly enjoy watching or participating in sado-masochistic ritual.

Language is a system of symbols used to communicate. These symbols can be spoken or written words, signs or pictures, movements or expressions. A language might be widespread or specific to a particular group: consider the use of English (increasingly a global language) in contrast to advanced computer programming or Cockney rhyming slang. Of course, successful communication relies on shared meaning. However, meanings can change depending on context and use: think of words like 'wicked', 'bad' and 'hot'. In everyday interaction, the meaning of language is implicit and taken for granted: we do not have to think 'well, he said "hello" so what does that mean?'. It is in the instances where language can be misinterpreted that we are most conscious of meaning – 'What did it mean when she winked at me?'. These breakdowns in communication are a common cause of embarrassment and conflict.

Artefacts are any objects made, modified or used by people. Often referred to by social scientists as 'cultural material', they could be objects of fashion, food, artwork, technology, machinery, weaponry, jewellery, architecture, sport or leisure. Artefacts are a crucial element of culture, informing us about how people live or lived. Andy Warhol famously painted a Campbell's tin of soup as a commentary on the culture he lived in. Archaeologists and historians rely on artefacts to develop an understanding of previous cultures.

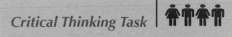

Critical Thinking Task

Consider the cultural artefacts depicted in the pictures below. With a partner, try to come up with some suggestions of what you believe they might tell us about the cultures they are taken from. Might they also tell us anything about values, norms, tastes and/or cultural roles? How informative are they in providing an insight into a 'way of life'? Try to think of three further artefacts that you believe tell us something important about your own contemporary culture.

Culture, power and resistance: the social production of meaning

Bocock ends his discussion of the meaning of culture by emphasising the social practices through which cultures are actively produced. This is an important development because it makes us recognise that cultures and cultural difference are not inherent or innate but constructed through human action. This is not to say that such construction is always deliberate or even conscious, but it opens up important questions concerning power and agency: who stands to gain if individual cultures elevate certain tastes or expertise over others? Who gets to decide what constitutes 'appropriate' behaviours or roles? Two further features to look out for when critically examining a specific culture are:

* the *institutions* which play a part in its (re)production, including branches of government, the media, organised religion and of course schools and the education system;
* the *opinion leaders* within society (who could be groups or individuals) that appear to have most power in shaping its contours, thereby influencing the way that others think and act and feel.

It is far too simplistic to claim that culture is made by those in positions of power and then passively experienced by 'ordinary' people. Culture is made through action, communication and shared experience. We all make culture when we interact with others, as we negotiate and construct shared interpretations and meanings. Much of our culture may be imposed 'from above', but it can also be made by people – and young people in particular – who do not hold positions of obvious power. Countercultures are an interesting example: they develop in opposition to mainstream culture. Throughout the second half of the twentieth century, youth culture was typified by countercultural groups: think of the teddy boys of the 1950s, the skinheads, mods and rockers of the 1960s, the hippies and punks of the 1970s, the new romantics and goths of the 1980s, and the ravers and gangstas of the 1990s. The ways that many of these youth countercultures were able to express defiance against the mainstream through their use of musical and fashion symbols is meticulously examined in Hall and Jefferson's seminal 1995 text *Resistance Through Rituals*.

But it has been questioned whether countercultures remain as significant today as they were. Two contradictory trends have taken place in the twenty-first century. On the one hand, there has been an emergence of new youth social movements that are explicitly oppositional, fighting pollution, industrial farming and corporate capitalism. For these dissenting voices, mass media and especially the internet have become powerful tools: they help mobilise and organise like-minded individuals and offer a platform through which their message can be seen and heard. 'Tactical Frivolity' and 'Reclaim the Streets' are two particularly spectacular current youth movements. Digging up sections of motorway and planting trees in the holes is an adventurous tactic for changing the collective mindset. Such grassroots 'culture making' has also been grasped by some very different groups in recent years: 'Fathers for Justice', 'Countryside Alliance' and 'Sarah's Law' offer contemporary illustration of this.

On the other hand, 'culture making' has been accompanied by a process of incorporation and commodification which began in the 1980s and has become increasingly powerful since. Countercultures can be appropriated by the mainstream and lose the subversiveness of their message as a result. Punk was the first and most prominent casualty: during the early 1980s their symbols and styles were taken up by commercial brands and retailers. When it became possible to buy dog collars and safety-pin jewellery, the original meanings of DIY and anti-consumer culture were lost. This commodification process might have accelerated in the twenty-first century, with the authenticity of countercultures like gangsta and rave questioned by academics (Redhead, 1993). And this is mirrored in wider culture as alternative lifestyle choices are undermined by big business: bands 'sell out' and 'go commercial', independent cinemas and record shops close and Starbucks cafes open everywhere.

Practical Task

One interesting recent phenomenon is 'culture-jamming'. Companies attempt to shape culture through advertisements. 'Culture-jammers' alter advertisements to subvert the messages. For example, a notice telling customers that their local bank branch was closing down had the slogan: *Because we care* scribbled underneath. Have a look at the Adbusters website (**www.adbusters.org**) and magazine. You can find lots of examples of billboards that have been sabotaged, as well as 'subvertisements' that spoof popular TV adverts.

'Culture-jamming' illustrates how messages can be interpreted differently and how individuals can shape culture. Try your hand at 'culture-jamming': identify an advertising campaign and try to creatively subvert the message.

Discussion of 'countercultures', 'culture making' and 'cultural commodification' demonstrate that the relationships between any individual and their culture(s) operate in more than one direction. They are, as Eagleton describes, an *immensely complex collaboration* between the two (2000, page 119). Culture is not an entity that exists independently of individuals, and nor is any one individual entirely defined by the culture – or cultures – to which they belong.

It is important to remember that individuals can:

* *interpret culture*: we experience, understand and engage with culture in different ways. So although culture implies shared and collective understandings, this does not entail homogeneity. One symbol of British culture today is the monarchy. But this does not mean that everyone in Britain aligns themselves with royalist sentiment. Rather, this aspect of our culture stimulates vigorous debate. For some, the monarchy is what puts that Great in Great Britain, for others it is a parochial and anachronistic monstrosity. And these types of divergent interpretation are commonplace. Ten guests at a party would tell different stories about that party, depending on their previous experiences, their relationships with others, who they talk to, their position within the group, their personality traits and their state of mind at the time;

and

* *shape culture*: culture offers a framework for how people are expected to think and act, but is, at the same time, redefined and maintained by peoples' individual and collective behaviour. The way that young people in particular have co-opted mobile phone and text message technology has introduced a whole new lexicon ('C U l8r', for example) and has created the phenomenon of 'happy-slapping', where violent episodes can be captured and shared by twenty-first century bullies. Both of these are innovations to which those 'in power' – the police and examination authorities for example – have had to respond.

Contemporary culture

Reflective Task

Many commentators argue that contemporary culture is quite distinctive from its predecessors (Giddens, 2002; Baudrillard, 2004). For instance, changes in communication and travel mean we now draw from aspects of cultures from around the world. An important question for you to consider is the extent to which you feel there is a coherent, shared and identifiable sense of culture today. Do the types of things you associate with contemporary culture tally with what others think?

Using the following headings, identify and make brief notes on what you consider to be the main characteristics of contemporary British culture:

* norms;
* values;
* beliefs;
* roles;

* tastes;
* language;
* institutions;
* opinion leaders.

Now share your initial thoughts within a small group. How many features appeared in more than one person's list? How far can you agree about key characteristics of British culture today?

From culture to cultures

From earlier discussions in this chapter you can see that identifying a single entity as 'contemporary British culture' is not an easy task, perhaps not even a possible one. A number of characteristics of late twentieth and early twenty-first century life have made it even harder still. For if culture is in large part about finding or creating shared understandings of *collective* experience, then how does it respond to rapid and widespread social, economic and political change, fragmentation and instability?

Many theorists have argued that it is no longer possible to talk about a singular 'culture'. Rather, they argue, society has entered a new stage, often referred to as 'postmodern'. Whereas culture might have been relatively stable, homogeneous and predictable in the past, postmodernists argue that this new stage is characterised by fluidity, plurality and diversity. From this perspective, culture has fragmented and become a site of contestation. Bauman (2000) coined the term *liquid modernity* to refer to the new and distinctive form that culture has taken. For him, as certainty and permanence disintegrate, relationships become increasingly unstable and temporary.

In fact, the idea that culture has become more fluid is not new. Friedrich Nietzsche, writing in the late nineteenth century, is often viewed as an early postmodernist. Certainly he argued that truth claims should be distrusted, that the distinction between reality and fiction has dissolved and that the culture could be characterised as nihilistic. These are all claims that sit comfortably within contemporary 'postmodern' thinking. Postman and Weingartner, in their seminal book *Teaching as a Subversive Activity*, of 1969, argued that *change changed* (page 23). Culture has always changed, but Postman and Weingartner's contention that the speed of change has dramatically increased is compelling. They use a metaphor of a clock to illustrate this. If 60 minutes represented the last 3000 years, the computer would have existed for the last five seconds and the satellite for the last second. Since the time of this book, the internet, email, laptop and PDA (personal digital assistant), mobile phone, budget airlines, satellite television have all come into existence (within the last 20 milliseconds!).

Many argue that these changes have impacted on the relationship between culture and identity. In the past, identity will have been quite tightly attached to just one culture: people were defined by the small number of communities or social groups they belonged to. Within the contemporary period, identity is much more loosely connected to group membership. People belong to a multitude of cultures, and their identity is likely to be different in each one. But the extent of this belonging is only ever partial and temporary. Contemporary culture is so fast-moving and exciting that people do not want to be tied to one 'way of life'. Rather we float around, temporarily attaching ourselves to attractive cultures before moving on.

From this perspective, the way that individual identity interacts with culture has moved from subcultural membership to neo-tribal affiliations. Membership of a subculture involves ascribing to the fixed norms and values of that subculture. Identity is defined by this membership. 'Neo-tribes' offer far more loose connections (Bennett, 1999). Associations have become increasingly fluid, partial and temporary. Today, identity is furnished with the wide range of cultural experiences and affiliations a person has, rather than being prescribed by the culture of the social group one aligns oneself to. An analogy that is frequently used to illustrate this is the child in the sweet shop. While the child of the twentieth century would have purchased a bag of their favourite sweets, the child of the twenty-first century can make their own bag of sweets from a wide array of choices. As such, contemporary culture prioritises freedom and choice.

However, this perspective has also been heavily criticised and it remains very much open to contest how free all individuals are to 'pick and choose' their cultural affiliations and identities. Equally, encountering choice and difference is not always experienced as a positive or empowering thing. For some it represents unwelcome change and disorientating uncertainty.

Characteristics of contemporary culture

In spite of these trends towards fragmentation and multiplicity, there appear to be a number of characteristics that are sufficiently common to reflect a shared contemporary culture. Some are especially salient with regard to reflecting on the nature of learning today.

- *Individualism*: since the 1980s, Western cultures have become increasingly centred around the interests of the individual. The fragmentation of social groups and community bonds is viewed by many as the main cause of antisocial behaviour.
- *Consumerism*: today, consumers do not simply buy because they *need* to, they buy because they *want* to. It is perfectly feasible to live with one or two pairs of shoes, yet some people feel they need 20 or more. Hence terms like 'shopaholic', 'BOGOF' (buy one get one free), 'impulse buying' and 'retail therapy' are becoming part of our common lexicon. Moreover, within consumerism, value is reduced to economic value. 'Shopping around' for the 'best deal' becomes the prevailing mindset in all social settings and relations.
- *Globalisation*: there has been a considerable increase in movement and co-operation between nations. This has been reflected in economic spheres (think of the World Bank, multinational companies, international trading), political spheres (with the creation of organisations such as the EU, UN and G8) and cultural spheres (as regards fashion, music, film, TV, foods, and other leisure activities). Migration between countries has led to many nations becoming 'multicultural'. At the same time, the dominance of the USA as an exporter of culture, has led many to refer to globalisation as a form of cultural 'imperialism': McDonalds, Coca Cola, Nike and the television series *Friends*, for example are brands easily recognised across the globe.
- *Technophilia*: the influence of – and our reliance on – technology has also increased tremendously. Even 10 years ago it would have been difficult to predict how central the email, text, mobile phone, laptop and PDA computer, SatNav, iPod and (most significantly) internet would become to our way of life today.
- *Internet hegemony*: it is difficult to understate the impact of the world wide web on culture today. It has become such an embedded part of culture that it is hard to imagine that Google began operating only in 1996, Wikipedia in 2001, My Space in 2003, Facebook in 2004, YouTube in 2005, and the web itself in 1993.
- *Democracy of fame*: it can sometimes appear that it is easier now than ever before to become famous, even without having any discernable talent. There are quick routes to (limited and temporary) fame through numerous internet sites like YouTube. Mass audiences are more and more accessible. Prime time television is saturated with programmes such as *Big Brother*, *Britain's Got Talent* or *Shipwrecked*, in which the audience becomes the star.
- *An emphasis on youth*: children and young people are much nearer to the centre of culture than previously. Their voices are more heard and more listened to. The emerging youth parliaments and school councils are acquiring greater power, and young people are becoming more adept at articulating their viewpoints. The British government's 'Every Child Matters' policy has prioritised the needs and concerns of children. The media has reflected (and some would say shaped) this shift in emphasis. Musicians and film and TV stars are generally far younger today than they would have been even 15 years ago. And young people are increasingly at the centre of the drama in popular series such as *Neighbours*, *Buffy the Vampire Slayer*, *Eastenders*, or *The OC*, where adults become 'child-like' supporting

characters in the background. Anti-aging creams and therapies have found a mass market as people try to fit in with a culture that celebrates youth.

• *The prevalence and significance of mass media*: increasingly, the general population's world view is enabled and constrained by the lens of the media. The majority of knowledge no longer derives from direct experience. Television, radio, film, music, internet and print media have become immensely powerful in shaping and defining our way of life. The media now rivals (and in many ways overwhelms) education as the source of information and knowledge in contemporary culture.

A crisis of culture?

Many social commentators have been led to conclude that contemporary culture is in a state of crisis. From this perspective, the current dominance of media in shaping and transmitting knowledge has resulted in a degradation of our cultural values, expectations and tastes. As Susan Sontag (1996) has argued:

the undermining of standards of seriousness is almost complete, with the ascendancy of a culture whose most intelligible, persuasive values are drawn from the entertainment industries.

Sontag, 1996

According to Wood, this is a post-intellectual era, in which we are experiencing a cultural transformation that is reversing four hundred years of intellectual evolution.

Wood, 1996, page 1

The following are often perceived as symptomatic of this 'dumbing down' process:

• style over substance;
• lightness over seriousness;
• self-centredness over communal sentiment;
• immediate over deferred gratification;
• popularity and financial worth defining value.

The potential implications for education and learning here are clear. In a 2006 survey conducted by the Skills Council, 1 in 10 of the 16–19 year olds interviewed suggested they would drop out of education if given a shot to become famous through the medium of reality TV.

Many would argue that the result of trends like these is a contemporary culture characterised by cynicism, blame, apathy, indifference and fear. There has been a proliferation of scare stories and moral panics, making people fearful of the food they eat, the air they breathe and the people they are surrounded by. People feel disconnected from each other: that they are living through social breakdown, that they can do little to make things better and that somebody else must be to blame. And much of this negativity is directed towards the young.

Young people are regularly associated with antisocial behaviour: their involvement with violence, gangs, alcohol and drug misuse is reported frequently. There has been a considerable rise in the number of young people criminalised since 2000: the high-profile emergence of Antisocial Behaviour Orders (ASBOs) and mosquito devices to disperse groups of 'undesirables' from public places add to this sense of a delinquent or 'feral' youth culture.

At the same time, and in spite of recent government initiatives, child poverty is extremely high in contemporary Britain: in 2007, the Department for Work and Pensions estimated that 2.9 million children lived below the poverty line. Recent UNICEF and Children's Commissioners' research has shown that Britain's children are among the least happy in the world. They suffer most highly from mental illnesses and feel most pressurised at school. One might argue that children today have lost the freedom they once would have had. Cultures of fear, concerned with issues including paedophilia, domestic abuse, internet and street safety, violence in media and video games, eating and unhealthy lifestyles, have resulted in ever greater restrictions: children have become 'infantilised'.

Learning in contemporary culture

Critical Thinking Task

Each of the dimensions of contemporary culture identified in the text has had an impact on learning today. Try to add to Table 1.1 below, identifying the way each shapes our understanding and practices of learning.

Table 1.1 Learning in contemporary culture

Features of contemporary culture	Impact on learning
Individualism	• Personalised learning and targets • Competition
Consumerism	• Learning arrangements framed in purchaser–provider terms
Globalisation	• Citizenship curriculum
Technophilia	• Use of electronic learning aids (e.g. interactive whiteboards)
Internet	• Reduction in non-exam-based assessment
Democracy of fame	• Growth and popularity of courses in media and film studies (and Beckham studies!)
Childhood and youth	• Policy focus on children's wellbeing and social and emotional development
Mass media	• To develop more interactive and stimulating learning experiences
Dumbing down	• Concern over rigour and quality of examinations
Multiple cultures	• Increasing range of educational choices and pathways

Looking at your completed table, discuss in your group the extent that contemporary culture provides more opportunities or threats for learning today.

Learning as a cultural activity

As has already been argued, learning does not take place in a vacuum. It is shaped by the environment it takes place within. We learn together, through communication. Sometimes that communication is two-way and conversational. At other times, it is one-way: we learn through reading, listening or watching. All these forms of communication are shaped by the dimensions of culture (including language, norms and tastes) identified above. As such, the very nature of learning is shaped by culture. Consider the following aspects of learning:

- *how we learn*: what are considered the most appropriate strategies to facilitate learning? Do we learn by listening or doing? By being quiet or communicating with each other? Do we learn by rote or through activity?
- *when we learn*: at what ages should learning take place? Should children start formal schooling at four or seven or somewhere in between? At what times of the day should people learn? What times of the year? And for how long?
- *who we learn from*: is a formal qualification necessary in order to legitimately help people learn? What should the teacher training involve? Can pupils and students learn from each other? Can older people learn from younger people?
- *who should learn*: should everyone learn the same things and in the same way? Should there be a discrete education for children born into higher social classes?
- *what we learn*: what subjects should be included on a curriculum? Should learning be divided into distinct subjects? Should there be an externally defined curriculum? Should it be content-led, skills-led, or competence-led?
- *where we learn*: can learning only take place within formal settings? Can we learn outdoors? Is leisure learning? Can we refer to watching television as learning? Does it depend on the type of programme we watch?
- *why we learn*: do we learn to improve our job prospects? To earn more money? For personal development? For knowledge acquisition? Because we have to? Or for reasons other than these?

So learning is not something that 'happens to' the learner in isolation. It cannot be reduced to a list of fixed psychological learner types as learning styles inventories tend to do. Neither can it simply be studied in its formal locations, without reference to its wider contexts. Learning takes place in the 'micro-level' interactions that occur within particular institutions, classrooms, friendship groups and teacher–pupil relationships. These comprise the 'cultures of learning' that mediate between formal educational structures and the learning experiences of individual students. James and Bloomer (2001) make use of the term *learning sites* to explain this:

Learning sites are also endowed with meanings – sometimes stable, sometimes contested, sometimes idiosyncratic and sometimes shared – that individuals bring to their learning and that they construct and reconstruct in the course of their learning. Moreover, they are situated within the wider social, cultural, economic, political and moral networks and have to be understood in terms of that situativity. Meanings and situativity change, not only between learning sites but from individual to individual and, in the individual case, from moment to moment.

James and Bloomer, 2001, page 2

Individual learners bring their own personal dispositions and prior experiences with them into a 'learning site'. These individual qualities mean that each pupil or student has a unique experience of the culture they interact with in that 'learning site'. And, through interaction, these unique experiences contribute towards the changing shape of the culture. As such, learning is:

- *situated*: clearly learning takes place in different settings. It is dependent on context. Everyone has had good and bad experiences of learning and these are largely dictated by situations and circumstances. These might be influenced by environmental contexts: the room is too hot, the view is too exciting, there is too much noise from the adjacent room, or the computers do not work. They might be shaped by the type of group: how long they have worked together, the skills and personality of the teacher, the dominant members, the activities they are involved in together;
- *relational*: learning experiences are dependent upon relationships. The relationship between learner and teacher is commonly found to be the key factor in the success or otherwise of learning. Relationships between peers are also highly important. Through continuously evolving interactions, members of the class learn what is expected of them. Essentially, they learn how to learn within that setting. The 'new kid' in the class has a very demanding task: needing to learn the culture of that class (the roles, expectations, values, language, tastes and so on) before being able to become a full participant;
- *dynamic*: learning changes. It is a process. An individual is the incomplete product of their combined learning experiences to date. Cultures of learning are constructed and reconstructed through interaction. The forms of learning that take place in the first week of term are very different from the first week after Easter. The learning of a child in her first week of school is entirely different from the same person's learning at A level or on a degree programme at university. Over the years, she will have been socialised into the culture of learning of her society: her previous schooling experiences have made her what she has become.

Practical Task

Because your learning is influenced and shaped by what is going on around you, your experiences will change in different settings. Think about your own experiences as a learner. Keep a 'learning log' over the period of a week. In it, try to reflect on the process of learning. Consider the kinds of contexts and relations that enable you to have positive learning experiences. As you write you might ask yourself some questions.

- What am I learning?
- Why am I learning it?
- Who is teaching/learning?
- Where and when is it taking place? Why?
- How am I learning and how do I know I am learning?
- What settings enable me to learn best/worst?

Characteristics of learning in contemporary culture

Although this chapter has demonstrated that 'contemporary culture' is not an easily identifiable or quantifiable thing, there are a number of sufficiently common characteristics that can be usefully identified. These offer both new opportunities and new obstacles for learning today. There are many reasons to feel optimistic about the state of learning in contemporary culture. There are also reasons for pessimism. Many of these characteristics will be examined in greater depth during the book. At this stage, let us briefly identify six reasons to be hopeful and six reasons to be concerned:

Optimism

- *Understanding what learning is*: recent theories of emotional intelligence and multiple intelligences have helped to widen our understanding of learning, once narrowly defined as knowledge acquisition.
- *Importance of learning to society*: contemporary employment requires education and training and this has resulted in massive investment and an emphasis on the value of learning.
- *Focus on stimulating learning experiences*: trainee teachers are encouraged to think about facilitating engaging learning through active, experiential learning and so on.
- *A greater focus on childhood*: there has been a growing emphasis on early years and preschool education, including extended schooling and SureStart. Society's responsibility towards all children has been indicated in 'Every Child Matters'.
- *Education for everybody*: through 'widening participation' and 'lifelong learning' agendas, government has attempted to construct a 'learning society', in which learning can take place inside and outside of formal education. As part of this focus there is now a greater requirement for employers to provide continuing professional development opportunities.
- *Wider opportunities for learning*: new learning opportunities have been created through globalisation, mass communication and technological advances. This has led to more opportunities to make use of information technology to experience and interact with the world.

Pessimism

- *A culture of assessment*: Many fear a curriculum that is stifled by over-examination. SATs, GCSE, AS and A levels mean children and young people are preparing for exams through much of their formal schooling.
- *Surveillance*: teachers and learners are watched more today than ever before and the results of surveillance are transparent (through published data such as league tables).
- *Quality assurance*: one consequence of increased surveillance has been the centralisation of quality assurance. To an extent, this has defined learning as outcome based (as measured by quantifiable performance indicators).
- *Fear*: a 'culture of fear' restricts behaviour and prevents people from taking risks. Parents are scared for the safety of their children, schools limit their curriculum through fear of litigation (e.g. field trips), teachers fear inspection and league tables. This can lead to restrictive 'teaching to the test'.
- *Anti-learning culture*: a significant dimension of youth culture today is that learning is 'uncool'. Truancy rates remain high, many teachers find classroom management very difficult and the number of young people continuing into post-compulsory education remains relatively low. There are significant numbers of young people who are totally disconnected from schooling.
- *Inequality*: despite repeated changes to the structure of formal schooling, education still reproduces a culture that justifies advantage and disadvantage. Inequality is normalised in a system premised on the idea that there are winners and losers (good grades = high-paid jobs).

Chapter Summary

After reading this chapter, you should recognise that:

- There are many interconnected meanings and uses of the word 'culture' – most straightforwardly it is the range of norms, values, tastes, languages, beliefs, artefacts and roles that constitute a 'way of life'.
- Contemporary culture is a different kind of thing to its predecessors – it has become less predictable, and more fluid, fragmented and plural.
- Depending on your viewpoint, this emergent culture is either fast-paced and exhilarating (with numerous exciting choices and opportunities) or hedonistic and nihilistic (in a state of superficial 'dumbed-down' meaninglessness).
- Contemporary culture offers both threats and opportunities for engaging learning.
- An understanding of learning as a cultural activity is vital for teachers and policy makers.
- Children and young people are 'experts' in contemporary culture – making use of this expertise in the classroom can give subject–content relevance, can enable pupils and students to actively participate in class and can help to develop self-confidence and self-esteem.

Research focus

Background

Arguably the definitive characteristic of contemporary culture (and the thing that sets it apart from any other) is the dominance of mass media. Any attempt to examine learning today must take account of media:

- as a source of learning material;
- as an alternative source of knowledge and information;
- as shaping the interests and expectations of learners;
- as reflecting the characteristics of contemporary culture.

Read the following book review and consider how accurate media representations of learning are likely to be. What factors might distort these representations?

- Scanlon, L (2008) How real is reel? Teachers on screen and in the classroom. *Australian Review of Public Affairs*, September 2008 **www.australianreview.net/digest/2008/09/scanlon.html**

Children and young people on screen

Many recent films have tackled childhood and adolescence in contemporary culture (both inside and outside formal education). These provide invaluable material to examine how these age groups are popularly constructed and presented. They frequently offer the audience a viewpoint of the world from the perspective of young people, highlighting the issues and problems they confront. Consider how childhood and youth are portrayed and examined in different films – as well as through other forms of media. You might find three films especially interesting:

- *Show Me Love* (1998; Swedish);
- *Ghost World* (2001; USA);
- *Kidulthood* (2006; UK).

Learning and culture on screen

A number of recent films and TV series have also explored learning and teaching within contemporary culture. Two that particularly caught the attention of educationalists were *Dangerous Minds* (1995) and *The Faculty* (1998). Read Giroux's article:

* Giroux, H (1997) Race, pedagogy, and whiteness in *Dangerous Minds*. *Cineaste*, 22 (4): 46–49.

Now try to analyse more-recent films and TV portrayals of learning and teaching. You should look at:

* *Freedom Writers* (2007);
* *Happy Go Lucky* (2008);
* *Teachers* (2001–2008).

Chapter 2

Lessons in culture, community and change: an historical account

Learning outcomes

By the end of this chapter you should be able to:

- provide historical illustration that learning and innovation have influenced social and cultural change;
- describe continuities and transformations in the ways learning has been perceived, valued and organised by human cultures of the past;
- account for the importance of education in constructing communities including contemporary nation-states;
- assess dominant understandings of the relationship between learning, education and the idea of 'progress'.

Chapter outline

In many respects, relationships between learning and culture are as old as all of human history. Established generations have always passed onto the young their accumulated knowledge of how best to live in the world. Children are not simply born possessing this information: 'culture' is something that needs to be learned. But the skills and competencies valued by hunter-gatherer parents living several thousand years ago are not those that a twenty-first century parent in Britain is likely to privilege. In the same way, many of the capacities and capabilities we now take for granted would have been alien to our first ancestors. Knowledge is culturally shaped and culturally communicated: its form and content vary in different parts of the world and over time. As human cultures change, so do dominant conceptions of what and how we learn. In this chapter you will explore the transition from the informal acquisition of knowledge in the earliest human societies to the institutionalised and highly regulated formal systems of education that dominate today.

Learning has also performed an historically important role in drawing boundaries around specific cultures and in constructing 'community'. Over the last 200 years, the introduction of compulsory schooling across Western Europe has helped to create the most common contemporary political community, the nation-state. In fact, this chapter argues that education and nationalism were very closely connected projects of the period of European history characterised as 'modernity'.

Again, relationships between learning and culture are dynamic, complex and potentially contradictory. Certainly, it is through learning that established values, beliefs and expectations are reproduced to continue into the future, but learning can also lead to innovation, discovery and ultimately cultural change. At different points in history, learning has been celebrated by some and feared by others as an engine of cultural transformation. Elsewhere it has been fought by some and defended by others as an instrument of cultural conservation or control. Indeed, 'change' itself has been conceived and responded to in a variety of ways, with significant consequence for the esteem (or otherwise) in which learning is held.

Reflective Task

Spend a moment thinking about your own skills and competencies. Which things that you know, or have learned how to do, do you consider most important? Why? Can you make a list of all those that you feel would be most fundamental to pass on to a future generation? Would you be able to teach these skills or would you need to rely on someone else's expertise? Imagine yourself as the hunter-gatherer and twenty-first century parents described in the introduction. What would your lists look like then? Compile a list from each perspective. How do they compare? How many different things does an individual need to know to live confidently and competently within contemporary culture?

Culture and learning: from 'simple' to 'complex'?

When attempting to tell a single story of human history, social theorists and philosophers – especially those from the West – often suggest that over time, human societies, human cultures and human systems for learning have become increasingly sophisticated and complex (see for example Giddens, 1991). In the 'simplest', earliest societies, the cultural knowledge that was passed on from adults to children was relatively straightforward. The skills and understandings needed – to communicate with other group members, to hunt animals or gather edible plants, to find shelter or to take part in shared rituals – could be taught and learned informally, primarily through observation and imitation. Neither the form nor the content of learning was the cause of too much consideration or concern; people learned to do what people had always done before (Lawton and Gordon, 2002). Children would accompany their elders on hunting trips for example, watching adult behaviour and, when appropriate, they themselves would take part. Additional learning was oral, through collective story-telling and day-to-day interaction with others from the group. Within many communities, there existed a gendered division between some forms of labour, with men and boys performing certain tasks, and women and girls performing others. By and large however, the same skills were shared and could be taught and learned by any member of the group.

In today's society, it is considered that our lives are much more complicated than that. The cultural knowledge we have accumulated is now too wide, too extensive and too disparate to be learned informally in this way. Formal institutions for learning such as schools, colleges and universities are required, as are specific individuals who are trained to teach. Within compulsory education, abstracted general principles are taught in favour of concrete and contextually specific skills: it is more important to be able to read the time from a clock-face for example, than to know precisely when a herd of deer is likely to be visiting a particular watering hole. And today a multitude of different roles or occupations can be performed within one cultural community. Not everyone is expected to know *everything*: farmers, bankers, astronauts and ballet dancers need rather different skills. Contemporary knowledge is increasingly organised into disciplines and subdisciplines. Specialist 'experts' are deferred to and relied upon in specific fields.

But what do we know about how such transformations have taken place? And *why* do human cultures change? Do they always change for the better? What is the role of learning here? Such questions have provided the stimulus for much intellectual and philosophical debate and it would be foolhardy to expect to provide many concrete answers here. However, it is possible to identify certain innovations – new skills developed or understandings acquired by our ancestors – which seem to relate to periods of significant change. It is also possible to examine critically other people's explanations of what propels human history and the stories they tell of how we have arrived at today.

Theories of social change

Over the last three centuries, the idea of progress has been centrally important: it has regularly been suggested or assumed that cultures change because human beings and their societies are striving to 'get better' and that the relationship between the past and the present – and the present and the future – is one of constant improvement. This implies that human history could be conceived in the shape of an ever upward-reaching path as depicted by Figures 2.1, 2.2 or 2.3.

There are clear reasons why such a perspective might have very popular appeal. However, many scholars argue that the notion that things change to get better – or *must* change to get better – is in fact a relatively recent way of looking at the world (Marx and Mazlish, 1996; Wright, 2006). It is also far from impartial: from this perspective it would appear that those cultures that demonstrate the most extensive or most rapid transformations are 'better' – more advanced/sophisticated/efficient – than those that appear to stay the same. It is perhaps not

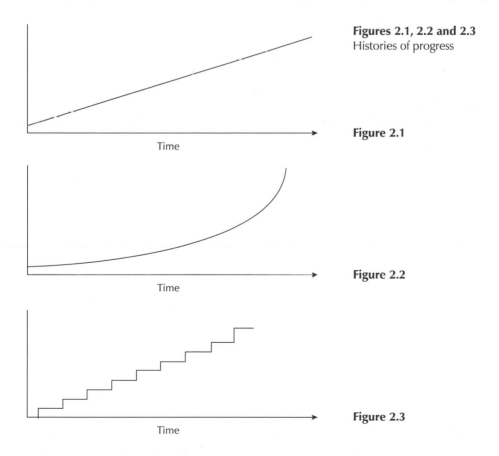

Figures 2.1, 2.2 and 2.3
Histories of progress

Time

Figure 2.1

Time

Figure 2.2

Time

Figure 2.3

surprising then that the notion of progress became increasingly popular and widely held during the eighteenth and nineteenth centuries and in Western Europe: this was a period and region in which human societies were experiencing especially rapid transformations in all areas of economic, political, technological and cultural life.

Historically, there have in fact been a number of alternate ways of conceiving social and cultural change. Like the passage of the seasons or the orbit of the moon, in the classical civilisations of Ancient Greece and Rome for example, the history of humanity was most commonly considered in terms of recurring cycles of growth and decline. Human cultures were expected to have a life akin to living creatures: they were born, would mature, decay and ultimately die out or fade away to be replaced by others with life-cycles of their own. Although individuals might be encouraged to pursue their own intellectual development, there was no necessary expectation of guaranteed improvement in the lot of all humankind. Were we to try and depict the 'shape' attributed here to human history, it might look a little more like Figure 2.4.

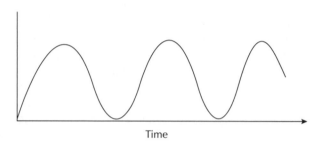

Figure 2.4 Cycles of growth and decline

Throughout much of Medieval Europe on the other hand, Christianity offered a rather different story of change. Following humanity's fall from grace in the eyes of God, and expulsion from the Garden of Eden, history was largely conceived in terms of degeneration. Likewise, after the fall of the Roman Empire and the end of Ancient Greek civilisation, until the Renaissance, it was considered by many commentators that the 'Golden Age' of human endeavour – of scholarship and innovation – was a thing of the past. In both cases, the 'shape' of this rather more pessimistic conception of social change and human history could be depicted as in permanent decline (Figure 2.5).

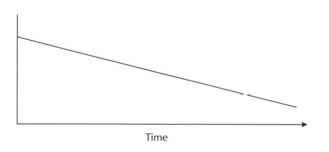

Figure 2.5 A history of decline

> ### Practical Task
>
> Identify what you consider to be ten key events or episodes from the last 2000 years of human history and arrange them on a piece of paper chronologically (in the order that they took place). If you choose to, you could focus on the history of one specific country or region of the world. Do the events you have chosen appear to tell a story of progress or of degeneration? Or is it difficult to tell? What events would you choose if you wanted to tell a story of progress? What about of degeneration or decline? Using Figures 2.1–2.5 as a starting point, try to depict your own illustration of the shape of human history. You may have noticed that in each of the figures, the y or vertical axis is unlabelled. Why do you think that may be?
>
> What is the implication for learning and education of each of these different ways of conceiving social change?

Both cyclical and degenerative theories continue to be held by different groups and individuals. However, the 'history as progress' story popularised by the European Enlightenment – a period located by competing commentators during the seventeenth, eighteenth and nineteenth centuries – came to dominate (Nisbet, 1980). It was this understanding that provided the foundations for the 'new' social scientific disciplines of sociology and anthropology, and this understanding that continues to inform much popular and academic argument today. As you will see, the notion of progress was also to have profound effect as regards the cultural value placed upon knowledge, learning and, ultimately, schools.

Theories of 'progress'

In order to understand the significance of the Enlightenment, it is necessary to acknowledge the social, cultural and political conditions that preceded it. At the risk of grossly over-simplifying considerable variation over both time and space, the term 'the Middle Ages' has been used to describe the period in European history following the decline of the Roman Empire in the fifth century right up until the sixteenth century. For much of this time, as David Hartley describes, the world appeared *a dark and dangerous place* (1997, page 7). Widespread and continual warring, public disorder, pestilence and plague ensured that life expectancies were short. Very few people received any form of schooling and most were entirely illiterate. Religion, astrology and superstition provided explanation and meaning in people's lives. Exploitative relationships between landowners and peasant farmers and between monarchs and their subjects went largely unopposed on the basis of faith in interpretations of Christianity, which bestowed 'divine' rights and authority to those in positions of power.

The Enlightenment on the other hand sought to replace 'blind faith' in religion and tradition with rational and methodical reasoning. Science and scholarship would bring 'light' to the darkness of ignorance and irrationality which had existed before. Drawing inspiration and encouragement from the groundbreaking theorisations of scientists such as Isaac Newton, Enlightenment thinkers began to conceive of the universe as a system that was ultimately knowable and understandable – graspable through human intellect. Mankind would no longer need to rely upon interpretations of religious teachings or folklore for explanation of this world: through systematic observation, calculation and experimentation, its actual workings could be discerned. Moreover, it was believed that if human beings could understand the world, they would be better positioned to influence it, to 'master' it and to control the direction of future change.

The seventeenth, eighteenth and nineteenth centuries were therefore a period of increased confidence and optimism in what humans, and in particular Western Europeans, could achieve. Science and reason appeared to offer illimitable promise for improvement. 'Knowledge' was an extremely valuable resource, to be accumulated and built upon to better the lot of humankind (Harvey, 1989). Learning and education began to assume especially high status. Such was the enthusiasm for reason, objectivity and the discovery of natural laws and universal principles, that scientific methods – observation, categorisation and experimental theorising – were applied to social and cultural life, not only the physical world. It was at this point that the modern 'social sciences', including the disciplines of sociology, anthropology and modern geography, were born (Hamilton, 1996).

Understanding others

Ancient Egyptians first built seaworthy ships some 5000 years ago, and since then human populations have travelled the globe, adventuring, migrating or invading, and in each case encountering people and places with ways of living different from their own. Throughout the thirteenth to sixteenth centuries, the exploratory expeditions of Marco Polo, Christopher Columbus, Vasco da Gama and others had significantly expanded Europeans' knowledge of the wider world. However, it was during James Cook's voyage to the Pacific in 1769 that the Enlightenment principles of scientific enquiry began shaping exploration and discovery, for on board Cook's ship were scientists and illustrators to systematically record, catalogue and classify everything that they encountered on distant shores. The wealth of material, information and 'evidence' that the first social scientists could build their theories from was dramatically increased.

How were they to make sense of the vast variety in human culture that international exploration revealed? Where nature's cycles and the biblical story of the expulsion from Eden had provided earlier blueprints for interpreting human history, Enlightenment commentators looked to their new 'religion' of science.

Evolutionary theories such as those popularised by Charles Darwin in *The Origin of Species by Natural Selection* offered particular inspiration. But where Darwin recorded and theorised around variation in species of plant and animal life, the so-called 'social Darwinists' attempted to apply similar models to groups of humans too. They tried to argue that different forms of cultural community could be ordered as a series of stages along an evolutionary scale, each an improvement on – or progression from – those that had existed before. Social change was explained and conceived in developmental terms, echoing the optimism – and arguably arrogance – that characterised much of Western European life. From this perspective, Western European cultures – of which the social Darwinists were themselves a part – represented the pinnacle of human endeavour so far, as illustrated in Figures 2.6 and 2.7.

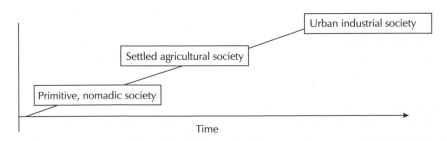

Figure 2.6 Progress in human society?

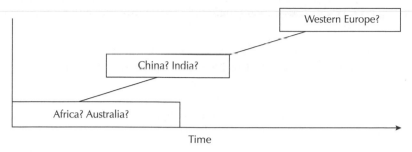

Figure 2.7 Locating places in time?

Problems with 'progress'

Aside from their obvious Eurocentrism, social Darwinist, or social evolutionist theories contain a number of spurious understandings and limitations. Much of the problem stems from their attempt to tidy or organise the enormous variety of human experience into a single, consistent and continuous story. This confuses relationships between geographical space and historical time. For the alternative cultures and social systems that Western Europeans encountered and sought to account for were not simply recognised as 'different' but were positioned *behind* Europe, as '*under*developed' or 'primitive' and as 'contemporary ancestors' of those in the West. Those cultures that exhibited most congruence with Western European expectations of how society should be organised were positioned higher up the evolutionary ladder than those that seemed most primitive or 'savage' from a European point of view.

Only one possible trajectory for all human societies is presented or admitted in such a Eurocentric view: the path societies will – or *should* take – is predetermined. Just as an acorn contains within it the potential to be an oak tree – and *only* an oak tree, not a fir tree or a daffodil or an elephant – the collective life of all humanity is predetermined to eventually take the form of the 'modern', urban and industrial democratic societies found in the West. Some cultures had just arrived at their potential more quickly than others. An oak tree will not grow so readily if an acorn falls in the wrong sort of environment, if it does not have the right soil, or lives through a drought, or if the acorn itself is damaged or defective in some way. Alternative, 'primitive' cultures were thus conceived in terms of 'stunted' or 'thwarted' growth.

The notion that there is only one ideal form that all human societies should strive to achieve is a deeply contentious and problematic one. In recent years there have been several criticisms of this approach.

- By suggesting that 'progress' in one predetermined direction is as natural and inevitable as the growth of an acorn into an oak tree, evolutionary theories commonly fail to award any significant attention to the particular social, political, economic and/or environmental contingencies that may have encouraged specific innovations in different parts of the world.
- As a consequence, they are only able to offer limited and unconvincing explanation for why some cultures appear to have 'progressed' more rapidly along the evolutionary ladder than others. This misleadingly suggests that Western Europeans must inherently be an especially inventive and progressive bunch.
- Progressive theories also depend upon a partial and selective reading of historical and geographic difference, often entirely ignoring, discounting or misinterpreting that which is most unfamiliar or appears most difficult to understand. Late twentieth-century anthropologists, for example, became very critical of the ways in which their disciplinary forebears had *mistakenly* interpreted others' cultures as 'simple' or 'primitive' because they could not see or could not understand the ceremonial, story-telling and other traditional practices

through which complicated cultural understandings could be transmitted and shared (see for example Rosaldo, 1989).

Of course, such theories also assume that there is a consensus as to what 'progress', 'improvement' or 'the right direction' mean. The dominant European perspective of the Enlightenment period tended to place value upon things like growth, profit, technology, industry, efficiency and mastery of the world. More recently, critics have argued that humankind might do better if notions such as stability, harmony, contentment, equilibrium or happiness were prioritised instead (Wessels, 2006). Ironically, progress itself cannot be measured or recorded scientifically but is based upon deeply subjective perspectives. Progressive theories look for and find evidence of 'progress' only where the values *they* value are shared.

This has important consequences for learning and the way that education is practised and organised. It could be argued that modern conceptions of reason, knowledge and progress have undermined and ignored the learning potential of alternative ways of apprehending and understanding the world.

Practical Task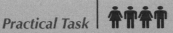

Aboriginal and Torres Strait Islander communities in Australia provide a good example of cultures that initially appeared 'primitive' through Western European eyes. Using resources in your nearest library or on reliable internet sites, begin some preliminary research on indigenous Australian cultures. Imagine yourself as one of the first white settlers to encounter these communities. What initial observations might lead you to describe the people you saw and their culture as 'primitive'? On the basis of your research, what evidence could you use to challenge that judgement? Share your reflections with others in a small group. Your collective research could be used to compile a poster presentation focusing on 'Complexity in Aboriginal and Torres Strait Islander Life'.

Can you envisage any challenges or obstacles that children from these communities might encounter if asked to attend a contemporary, formally organised, primary or secondary school?

When considering change, it is important to recognise these potential pitfalls and to be wary of the many pervasive and persuasive assumptions about progress that are still very regularly made. In particular, it is inadequate to rely on progress – as a 'natural' or inherent impulse in humanity – as an explanation for change. Recognition and consideration must also be given to particular geographical and historical contingencies (Diamond, 1997). And it must also be acknowledged that *all* historical accounts – including this one – are partial, selective and incomplete.

Innovation, learning and change

With this in mind, the remainder of the chapter provides a very loosely sketched outline of some especially significant innovations in learning and explores their relationship to social and cultural change. Here 'innovation' refers simply to the introduction of something new – a new skill, new perspective or new understanding. Such innovations cannot be conceived as simply appearing from nowhere. They emerge from, or are a response to, specific historical and geographic contexts. In each case it is instructive to consider factors such as the physical environment, rate of population growth and existing economic and/or political structures, as well as dominant belief systems and values that characterise a particular place and time.

In terms of historical analyses, it is not always possible to conclusively establish the causality of relationships between innovation, already existing cultural systems and change. Archaeologists tell us that several thousand years ago, our ancestors learned to fashion a stick to dig and prepare the land for crops, an innovation which would later lead to the development of the plough. They cannot tell us however, whether those ancestors were purposefully looking for a way to tame their physical environment and harness its resources (perhaps the food they could find from foraging was insufficient, and hunting and gathering was making them tired) or perhaps it was only accidently discovered that hitting solid earth with a stick-like object would change its properties in such a way that specific plants were encouraged to grow.

What *is* clear is that a change or innovation in any one part of the system can have much wider consequence; each of the factors that influence the cultural system in Figure 2.8 – the physical environment, demographics, economic and political structures and values and beliefs – are closely and complexly interdependent. Intentional or otherwise, the invention of the plough and the birth of agriculture drastically altered the economic and political structure of once nomadic, now settled, human groups. It also permitted rapid population growth, transformed great swathes of the physical landscape and created a *new* cultural system and context from which *new* innovations would ultimately emerge.

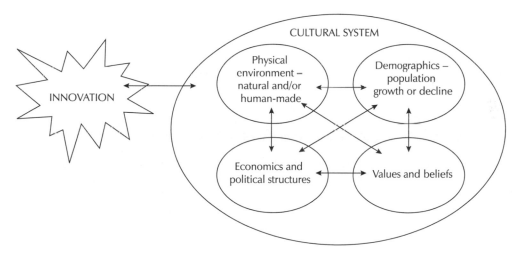

Figure 2.8 Innovation and culture

Critical Thinking Task

Consider the following list of inventions and innovations. On your own, identify and rank in terms of importance the three that you consider most significant in terms of social and cultural change. Under the headings 'Possible stimulus' and 'Possible consequence', make notes for each of your chosen three innovations suggesting their relationship to the physical environment, demographics, economic and political structures and/or values and beliefs. In a small group, compare your lists, taking turns to explain and justify your selection of the single most significant innovation in human history. Which additional innovations might you want to add?

- The controlled use of fire
- The invention of the wheel
- The production of paper
- The complex abacus
- The production of the first mechanical clock
- The invention of the printing press
- The invention of the microscope
- Vaccinations
- The invention of the steam engine
- The first camera
- The recording of sound
- Radio transmission
- The first assembly line
- The first computer
- The internet
- Space exploration

Language and community: the significance of speech

The invention and mastery of tools such as the plough, the spear, the steam engine or the personal computer have each been hugely influential in transforming our social, cultural and physical worlds, as have innovations in knowledge such as the discovery that diseases can be caused by bacteria, or that the earth is a sphere. However, discussion of transformatory innovations ought really to begin with an even more fundamental human adaptation and ability – the capacity to use language to communicate (Sapir, 1921).

Language acquisition is also vitally important for the transmission of culture: it facilitates the abstract forms of thought and communication that distinguish humanity from monkeys and the great apes. Our language enables us to share, to recognise and to collaboratively build upon meanings, understandings and interpretations of the world. It also plays a crucial role in the construction of community. For not only one language has developed through history, but a multiplicity. Each language invites and enables those who use it to identify themselves as part of a group among whom personal sets of meaning, interpretation and experience are likely to be most closely shared. As such, it stands as a boundary marker for cultural sameness and difference, constructing 'insiders' and 'outsiders' – those people who are most and least 'like me'.

This is not to argue that language and culture are exactly the same: it is perfectly possible that a single cultural community can comprise a number of different linguistic groups, for there are other ways in which important understandings can be shared. The norms, values and belief systems described in the previous chapter are not necessarily dependent on communication through the same spoken words. Nonetheless, linguistic diversity is often encountered and presented as an obstacle or challenge to cultural stability. Where native language is not shared by all community members, alternative ways of recognising commonality may need to be purposefully forged.

Practical Task

The history of the Welsh language and its use in schools in Wales provides an interesting illustration of the relationships between language, cultural identity and formal education. Using resources collated by organisations like The National Library of Wales (**www.llgc.org.uk**), BBC Wales (**www.bbc.co.uk/wales/history**) and the Welsh Language Board (**www.byig-wlb.org.uk**), research answers to the following questions.

- Why did the number of Welsh people speaking Welsh as their first language decline drastically during the nineteenth century?
- What was the 'Welsh Not'?
- How did Welsh communities and Welsh politicians respond to British government directives for education in Wales?
- What campaigns for Welsh education have been mounted during the last 100 years?
- How successful have these been?

Settlement, city life and social stratification

The earliest human social groupings were considerably smaller than today's. In a hunter-gatherer tribe of say only 100–150 people, it was perhaps automatic for individuals to feel kinship and affinity with those they recognised through regular face-to-face interaction as members of the same insider group. As human societies grew – both in terms of population size and over greater geographical distance – such affective kinship could no longer be guaranteed.

The transformatory impact of a tool such as the plough has already been discussed. Through learning how to cultivate crops – that is, in recognising that seeds could be taken from wild grasses and purposely planted on prepared land to provide a future food supply – human societies were encouraged and enabled to settle in a specific area for a prolonged period of time. It is therefore thanks to innovation in agriculture that urban and built environments first emerged.

The most successful of early settlements developed in close proximity to river systems: in Mesopotamia (modern-day Iraq), between the Tigris and Euphrates, in Egypt along the banks of the Nile and in China along the River Huang (Cunningham and Reich, 2005). Here, human populations devised ways to harness the resources of their natural environment. Not only did river systems provide alluvial soil rich in nutrients but, in the case of Sumerian Mesopotamia, they also provided the water that was used to develop the world's first artificial irrigation and plumbing systems.

Because agricultural innovation provided a comparatively stable and reliable food supply, it also correlated with a rapid explosion in population growth. However, proportionate to the human energy and input they demanded, early farming methods actually produced more food than was individually required. Not everyone would need to work the land, and a considerable surplus in labour and potential manpower was also produced. This was just as well, for the development of early settlements also involved the creation of entirely new tasks and jobs. The canal systems which provided irrigation for example, needed regular maintenance to prevent them from silting up and becoming blocked. As people opted to remain in one place indefinitely, they required more permanent dwellings to live and commune in: houses and early municipal or ceremonial spaces had to be designed and built. Likewise, as individuals were no longer responsible for producing their own food, new systems were needed to facilitate trade, taxation and exchange. And as larger populations require greater and more complicated governance than smaller ones, bureaucracy and bureaucrats were also born. Settlement resulted in social stratification, as not all of the roles performed by individuals were rewarded with the same level of status or wealth.

In summary, settlement led to what is now understood as the first 'civilisations'. Here civilisation refers to a social organisation which exhibits complexity regarding the variety of interdependent roles performed by different members of the group. Critically for our discussions, settlement also led to two vitally important innovations in learning: the development of written language and the emergence of formal education and schools.

Written records, literacy and the emergence of a cultural elite

As the size of communities grew, individual members could be separated by considerable distance. People could no longer rely on oral and face-to-face interaction to communicate information or share ideas. Furthermore, bureaucratic structures and new systems of commerce required a way of keeping record of agreements between individuals and of goods that had been exchanged. The first written languages – 'cuneiform' in the Sumerian Empire of Mesopotamia, and Egyptian hieroglyphics – developed in response (Fischer, 2004).

Also required were scribes and other clerics, able to write and to count and record. Unlike the skills of hunting and gathering, ploughing and planting, or building and digging – all of which could still be learned primarily 'on the job' – learning to read and write required specific and prolonged instruction, and so the profession of 'teacher' and the designated institutions 'schools' and 'education' were created at this time. But such instruction had to be regarded as an investment and would have cost a great deal in terms of both material resources and time. In both Sumerian and ancient Egyptian societies, only the male children of the most privileged were likely to receive a formal training – or 'education' – in school. The vast majority of both populations remained entirely illiterate. From the outset, education and literacy became a marker of status and a mechanism for reproducing inequalities of power and opportunity between individuals separated by rank or class.

Although it appears that written languages were initially conceived as an instrumental response to specific economic and administrative needs, their impact upon human culture has been much more extensive and profound. As written alphabets developed – employing symbols to represent individual sounds and syllables rather than to denote the meaning of specific words – text was used to capture, articulate and encourage the genesis of ever more complex and creative ideas. Written languages enabled the great intellectual scholarship and philosophical inquiry of ancient civilisations in India, China and Israel, as well as Greece and Rome.

But again, in most of these cases, literacy and scholarship were the preserve of only the most privileged. It was almost exclusively the thoughts and perspectives of the ruling classes that were recorded for future generations in the exalted form of 'classic' texts. And so it was that the seeds of a sharp distinction between 'high' (elite, finite, written and recorded) and 'low' (popular, everyday and ephemeral) cultures were initially sewn. 'Learning' for the illiterate majority continued to be informal, unregulated, and *ad hoc*, their languages and cultures still reproduced primarily through oral and embodied means.

The philosopher and anthropologist Ernest Gellner argued that, for most of human settled history, social life and learning were stratified such that cultural differences defined positions *within* society far more convincingly than they defined the limits around the whole of the social group (Gellner, 1996). Although the first empires of Mesopotamia, the Greek city-states of

Athens or Sparta, and the feudal kingdoms of Medieval Europe could each be accurately described as complex, single, social systems, they did not necessarily constitute single, coherent, *cultural* groups. The languages and high cultures that were recognised within formal education in each of these societies were largely divorced from the words spoken – and meanings shared – by everyday people on the street. Indeed, unlike the written word, which assumed a certain permanence once committed to paper (or clay or papyrus), oral languages were fluid, open to outside influence and subject to mutate, develop off-shoots or otherwise change. Gellner illustrates this by referring to a claim made by historian Eric Hobsbawn, that on the date that Italy was to become a unified nation – as late as 1860 – only 2.5 per cent of its resident population actually used the language officially recognised as 'Italian' when communicating day to day.

Both Gellner and Hobsbawm continue by arguing that linguistic and cultural diversity within social systems was not the cause of much concern to anyone until relatively recently. In feudal Medieval Europe, for example, those who ruled over kingdoms or manors did so on the basis of entrenched – and largely unchallenged – hierarchical authority. So long as their subjects continued to accept their lower ranking in the social order as inevitable – and so long as they continued to pay their taxes – it did not much matter who they considered their *cultural* community to be. But this was to change dramatically with the onset of 'modernity'.

'Modernity', compulsory education and the construction of the nation-state

As a point of clarification, when social theorists talk of 'modernity', they are not (in general) talking about the contemporary day. Confusingly, they are not always even talking about a specific period of time but rather a number of especially influential social practices and ideas that collectively came to represent a significant change in perspective, or disjuncture, from previous times. Critically, 'modernity' refers to a dominant outlook which had come to see the present as substantively different from the past: that is, where 'traditional' – '*pre*-modern' – society emphasised the reproduction of the past in the present, modernity emphasises instead development and change (Dupré, 2004). As such, it is intimately bound with the Enlightenment project and its values as already described. For our purposes, it is sufficient to draw attention to just some of the social, economic, political – and ultimately educational – transformations that the transition to modernity both reflected and entailed.

- 'Reason' and 'rationality' built upon 'objective', 'scientific' method were valued and promoted in place of superstition, prejudice and unquestioned faith. The premium placed upon knowledge was high.
- Progress and technological and intellectual innovation were promoted over stability, security and the reproduction of the status quo.
- Market economies replaced subsistence economies as wealth and financial prosperity were increasingly prioritised. Through processes of industrialisation, mechanisation and intensi-fied capitalism, economic growth began to dramatically exceed natural population growth, at least in the industrial and commercial centres of the world.
- As a consequence of changing labour market structures and modes of production, geographical and social mobility was also increased. Sons were no longer expected to work the same piece of land, perform the same role or occupy the same social ranks their fathers and forefathers had done before.
- The hierarchical power of church leaders and monarchs was significantly challenged. Feudal kingdoms collapsed across Medieval Europe, and in their place today's system of recipro-cally recognised sovereign and territorial nation-states began to emerge.

The impacts of such wider transformations upon education and learning have been profound and will continue to be explored in later chapters of this book. The Industrial Revolution and increased mechanisation of production, for example, demanded an ever-growing workforce who could, at the very least, master basic literacy and numeracy skills. And so, when the political and economic environment required it, the systems of formal instruction that had long remained the preserve of only the upper classes – or the charitable, but limited enterprise of a wealthy benefactor or religious group – were finally extended to provide an elementary education for all.

The combination of technological innovation and the emergence of capitalist market economies also led to a transformation in people's relationship with the written word. It has been emphasised that for much of its history, written language had been the preserve of a small number of religious scholars, rulers and the cultural elite. The invention of the mechanical printing press in 1440 began to change that (Anderson, 1983). Early books continued to be published in Latin – the language of the privileged – but within 150 years the market for Latin texts was almost completely saturated. Enterprising publishers looked to alternative ways to profit from printing as a commodity. The Protestant Reformation in Germany in the early 1500s was also significant. Martin Luther famously used vernacular German to produce a translation of the Bible. This was a very important step in democratising the written word. From then on, other texts began to be printed in everyday languages. With the Industrial Revolution and the development of the steam-powered rotary press, thousands of copies of written material – journals, newspapers and the new genre of popular fiction – could be printed within a single day.

'Imagining community'

The social scientist Benedict Anderson (1983) argues that 'print capitalism' played a crucially important role in the formation of the contemporary nation-state. Easy access to printed materials allowed disparate individuals who shared a vernacular language to 'imagine' themselves as part of a single community. An individual reading a daily newspaper, for example, would be aware that other people 'like him or her' were receiving exactly the same information at the same time. They were linked and united as an audience through their language, even if they knew they were never likely to actually know each other or ever meet.

If you recall Gellner's argument, prior to the modern period, the world was comprised of *complex, intertwined but not neatly overlapping patterns* of fluid, linguistic and cultural community overlaid by more permanently engrained hierarchies of power and rank. But with the rise of nationalism, it became conceived instead as a *world consisting of neat political units, systematically and proudly differentiated from each other* by something called 'national culture' and tied to a bounded geographical territory (Gellner, 1996, page 98). Governments were now concerned to demonstrate something akin to internal cultural homogeneity within the 'nations' that they took political responsibility for. For, after beginning to dismantle the 'blind faith' which had provided feudal monarchs with their power and authority, they needed to find some other claim to the legitimacy of their rule.

The relatively recent genesis of the modern nation – few dating back any further than the mid-nineteenth century – dispels the popular myth that any national identity is 'natural', ahistorical or innate. Remember that at their nation's inception, reputedly only 2.5 per cent of the population who from then on were considered 'Italian', actually belonged to the official Italian linguistic community group. Modern nations are, in fact, to a large extent, political constructions. The sense that a nation is comprised of 'people like me' has had to be purposefully produced.

Here the role of a formal system of compulsory education becomes key. What better method to communicate a shared official language, shared set of values and shared framework for understanding the world or to inculcate the feelings of belonging to, and identifying with, the national group? And so it was at the behest of *national* systems of government that free and compulsory education was extended beyond the limited provision religious organisations had been able to provide (Ramirez and Boli, 1987). In one famous study, historian Eugen Weber describes the processes through which, during the late nineteenth century, the extension of a standardised school system – using rather draconian measures of ridicule to police the language that pupils spoke in class – effectively *taught* a disparate peasant population to become the nation today recognised as France (Weber, 1976; see also Hearn, 2006).

'Modern' education and 'modern' childhood

We have already seen that in the 'pre-modern' world, for most people learning in pre-modern society was something that simply took place as part of day-to-day life. As Hartley tells us, *little cultural distinction was made between children and adults*. Because children learned through taking part in adult activity, they were therefore aware of, and often party to, nearly all aspects of adult life (Hartley, 1997, pages 8–9). However, during the late eighteenth, nineteenth and twentieth centuries, both learning and childhood were significantly transformed (Aries, 1996; Larochelle, 2007). Larochelle argues that, with the advent of what she describes as 'the school form' (that is, formal systems of compulsory education), learning through interpersonal relationships:

was supplanted by a pedagogical type of relationship that was founded on distance and isolation, in both physical and symbolical terms (Larochelle, 2007, page 715).

Such 'distance' and 'isolation' ensured that 'learning' came to be seen as something distinct and separate from everyday life and informal socialisation, and that 'childhood' was conceived as distinct and separate from adulthood. Larochelle continues by making the following important points:

- modern schools used systems of exercises and drills that were standardised and could be simultaneously delivered to all class members. This was very unlike the individual and personalised tuition that had gone before. Commercial printing was used to produce textbooks for further standardisation;
- learning was now something that happened in a location that was *specific (removed from life and kept at a safe distance from unsavoury places)* and *structured* with signs and restrictions informing children how to behave (*e.g. classroom furniture designed to make children maintain a certain posture; [. . .] the positioning of windows so as to keep all eyes focused on the business inside the classroom; the prominent display of moral urgings in poster for or on the blackboard* (Larochelle, 2007, page 715);
- learning took place within a specific schedule. It would happen at particular times of day on particular days of the week, and different subjects would be allocated their own slots within the course of children's study. Compulsory learning would also take place when students were a particular age;
- 'knowledge' was no longer the information and skills an individual simply needed to get by and play a part within society. Through written text, knowledge became *increasingly codified, objectified and disciplined* or abstracted. Learning was cut off from social frames of reference (Larochelle, 2007, page 716);
- school learning was concerned foremost with learning how to do things according to rules.

Vincent (1980) provides additional illustration of this final point:

Whereas previously, regardless of the field, an apprentice would, from the outset produce a piece of work, and thereafter several pieces of work until achieving a 'masterpiece', a schoolchild would, in marked contrast, be compelled not only to produce according to the rules (the result was no longer the only thing that counted) but would indeed be compelled to produce and re-produce drills and exercises whose object was the application of rules (Vincent In Larochelle, 2007, page 716).

Herein lies an inherent tension in the way that learning and education have been framed and utilised by modernity and the nation-state. For although modernity professes to value reason, science, knowledge and, above all else, progressive change, in attempting to hold together or produce a cohesive, national cultural community, the formal systems of national education we have inherited from this period, arguably promote conformity, consensus and compliance much more readily than they invite intellectual emancipation or revolutionary change.

Critical Thinking Task

In a 1996 article, Levinson and Holland suggest that we look at the *paradoxical potentialities of schooling* (page 22) as education can be conceived as both the engine of, and brakes upon, possible social and cultural change. Look out for – or find through the internet – newspaper stories reporting public and political debate concerning education. Listen out for audience phone-ins or politicians airing their perspectives on any educational matter, and in each case try to identify whether the progressive – and potentially transformatory – function of education, or its conservative function is being emphasised.

Chapter Summary

After reading this chapter, you should recognise that:

- Innovations in learning and culture are dynamically interrelated to specific places and times.
- Learning – and in particular language acquisition and literacy – performs a vital role in constructing and maintaining shared cultural communities.
- Literacy and formal systems of education have long been implicated in the stratification of social systems and the cultural reproduction of rank and class.
- During the period characterised as 'modernity', 'childhood' came to be more clearly distinguished from adulthood, and learning became a formalised and structured activity in which what, where and how individuals should learn became more tightly regulated and clearly defined.

Research focus

Background

Lawton and Gordon provide a useful historical overview by focussing on the emergence and development of key educational ideas and their relation to changing social contexts during the last 3000 years:

- Lawton, D and Gordon, P (2002) *A history of western educational ideas*. London: Routledge.

As its title suggests, the book concentrates its focus on the development of *'Western'* education but highlights the significant influence of non-Western and especially Islamic scholarship. This is an important consideration for your own further study as it is all too easy to reproduce Eurocentric perspectives when charting the history of ideas. Likewise, Reagan provides an alternative history of non-Western education, which you may like to use as a counterpoint to the histories presented here:

- Reagan, T (2008) *Non-western educational traditions: indigenous approaches to educational thought and practice*, 3rd edition. Lawrence Erlbaum: New Jersey.

Comparative histories

This chapter has only been able to provide the briefest and most general overview, but you could use historical material to research and examine or compare the relationships between learning, formal education and cultural identity in individual countries and over a specific period of time. How did the education system reflect and influence the cultural values and understandings of apartheid South Africa, for example, in Nazi Germany, or within Victorian Britain at the height of Empire? The following texts could be used as a starting point for such research.

- Abdi, AA (2002) *Culture, education and development in South Africa: historical and contemporary perspectives*. Cape Town: Bergin and Garvey.
- Lowe, R (ed) (1992) *Education and the second world war: studies in schooling and social change*. London: The Falmer Press.
- Mangan, JA (ed) (1988) *Benefits bestowed: education and British imperialism*. Manchester: Manchester University Press.

Education and progress revisited

The close association between education and progress is today still very influential in the realm of development studies and 'modernisation theory', where rates of literacy and attendance at primary school are regularly interpreted as measures of a nation's economic and political health. Follow-up research could offer a critical perspective on the assumptions about learning and culture made by development organisations such as the World Bank and IMF (International Monetary Fund), and explore how the historical experiences of Western societies are still used as a model for plotting *'under*developed' countries' future success. A useful introductory text is:

- Stephens, D (2007) *Culture in education and development: principles, practice and policy*. Oxford: Symposium Books.

Chapter 3

Learning in uncertain times: perspectives from philosophy

Learning outcomes

By the end of this chapter you should be able to:

- outline the claim that knowledge, morality and authority are more uncertain, fragmented, fluid, complex and pluralised in contemporary culture than at previous times;
- assess the extent that changes in the status and perception of knowledge impact on learning today;
- critically discuss the extent that education can transmit shared values and cultivate 'moral intelligence' today;
- examine the relationship between democratic classroom interactions and learning, particularly in theories and practices of 'student voice'.

Chapter outline

The chapter starts by outlining the characteristics that distinguish contemporary culture from previous periods: a heightened sense of fragmentation and fluidity, complexity, uncertainty and change. Within these new cultural settings, the chapter explores three related facets of learning: the most appropriate kinds of knowledge to be taught; moral education and common values; and classroom relations between teachers and learners.

- *Knowledge*: can we claim to know anything with certainty? What are the benefits of a sceptical outlook? How do changes in the construction and presentation of knowledge impact on learning?
- *Moral education*: does contemporary culture allow for the idea of a coherent set of moral rules that can be learnt? Should children be taught culturally prescribed values or be provided with opportunities to learn 'moral habits'? What values are shared within contemporary culture and how can teachers foster 'moral intelligence' in the young?
- *Teacher–learner relations*: how do teachers maintain authority over their subject/class? Can the principles of 'deliberative democracy' develop capacities in learners that enable them to cope with or embrace uncertainty, fluidity, plurality? What practices best cultivate effective 'student voice'?

It is not the intention here to provide an overview of philosophy over the last 3000 years. You will not be encountering the work of many philosophers as you read this chapter. To avoid a 'potted history' of the philosophy of education, we touch only briefly on the work of great philosophers. However, we believe that the works of two great philosophers are especially pertinent within the contexts of contemporary culture, and their work is considered in more detail here. These are the nineteenth-century German philosopher, Friedrich Nietzsche – who is frequently viewed as the 'prophet of postmodernity', and the twentieth-century American philosopher, John Dewey – who articulated the theories of pragmatism and progressivism that appear to fit well within contemporary cultural conditions.

Contemporary culture

Postmodern theorisations inform us that we have entered a new and distinctive age: that the homogeneity, stability and certainty of previous periods have dramatically disintegrated (Lyotard, 1984). And while there remains disagreement over quite the extent of that change (see Beck, 1993), it is evidently the case that contemporary culture possesses certain novel characteristics.

- *Fluidity*: Bauman considered the defining characteristic of contemporary life to be that nothing stands still – everything is ephemeral. He referred to this current period as *liquid modernity* (Bauman, 2000) to denote the speed of movement of people and ideas.
- *Plurality*: the movement of people and ideas around the world means that in many societies today a plurality of cultural influences and different ways of living co-exist. Britain for example is regularly described as 'multicultural', 'multiethnic' and 'multifaith'. Given this, perhaps it makes sense to talk of contemporary *cultures*, such is the multiplicity of lifestyles in existence today.
- *Fragmentation*: the norms that govern behaviour and social relations are increasingly open to contestation. Social life has become more atomised than in previous times: people lead very different lives from one another. As traditional constructs (including gender roles and class identities) break down, people become freer to live outside of existing social scripts.
- *Uncertainty*: the unpredictability of the fast-changing world makes it more and more difficult to make predictions. For many, this period of history is characterised by anxiety: fuelled by the precarious, insecure and uncontrollable nature of modern life (Bauman, 1997).
- *Complexity*: as a result of the above characteristics, the choices people make today are less straightforward. While it is easy to overstate how simple life used to be, living in contemporary culture involves making choices from a multiplicity of possibilities, without clearly defined parameters for behaviour, or coherent pathways to follow.

Changes in the structure of the modern Western world have heralded these cultural shifts. These include changes in the patterns of migration, economic, cultural and political globalisation, mass media communication, technological advances, increased affluence, and extensions in the numbers in further and higher education. Nevertheless, few theorists today claim that a modernist, enlightenment culture has been entirely superseded by plurality, fluidity, fragmentation, uncertainty and complexity. Enlightenment orientations, as outlined in the previous chapter, remain very significant but are now framed by heightened anxieties, complication and doubt. If we accept that these five characteristics are apparent in contemporary culture, and that they are the characteristics that make contemporary culture unique, the question of their combined impact on learning becomes pertinent.

The key implication for learning in contemporary culture is how authority is achieved and maintained. The combined impact of plurality, fluidity, fragmentation, uncertainty and complexity is the erosion of taken-for-granted authority. The authorities of objective knowledge, of absolute moral codes and of the status of the teacher have become increasingly open to contestation.

Learning about knowledge

Until relatively recently, knowledge obtained during a lifetime was derived almost entirely from direct experience. Essentially, there was less to 'know'. Aristotle is famously regarded as the last person who knew everything that could be known in his time – and that was nearly 2500 years ago! Since then, the amount of knowledge humanity claims has escalated enormously. For the majority of human existence, it would have been uncommon to know anything beyond the local community and environment. Today, a substantial proportion of knowledge is second hand. It is acquired via an intermediate – most commonly the mass media. People today claim knowledge of countries they have never travelled to, people they have never met, realities in space and inside atoms that they can never have experienced directly.

If the bulk of knowledge is gained through an intermediary, then it is dependent on high levels of trust. Sources of knowledge need to be (or at least seem) entirely reliable and trustworthy. Within contemporary culture, this has largely ceased to be the case. The authority of the priesthood, once the most elevated informant of knowledge in the UK, has been discredited by increased secularism and by stories of malpractice. Democratic leaders are pilloried daily by newspapers, television news and internet bloggers. Those same media outlets seem to be repeatedly caught out for peddling half-truths and outright lies. Even scientists, the most esteemed knowledge makers within contemporary culture, are blamed for global warming, pollution and the advent of new diseases. As such, contemporary culture displays cynicism towards today's knowledge makers: with education and the teaching profession being continual targets.

Reflective Task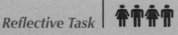

Today, we are presented with knowledge in a variety of forms and from a variety of sources. We have to think carefully about which knowledge claims we trust and which we doubt. Look at the following ten statements. Rank them in order – from the one you know most confidently to the one you know least confidently. Compare your individual ranking with the rest of your group and try to come up with an order that you can all agree on. Now compare the different statements. Write a list of what makes some of these statements more convincing than others and what makes you suspicious of certain knowledge claims.

- I know that I exist.
- I know that if I let go of my apple it will fall to the floor.
- I know that UFOs exist.
- I know that God exists.
- I know that Al-Qaeda is an evil terrorist organisation.
- I know that $2 + 3 = 5$.
- I know that Amy Winehouse is addicted to drugs.
- I know that stealing without need is wrong.
- I know that the cover of this book is yellow.
- I know that this book is a book.

Now discuss with your group what forms of knowledge are most commonplace within contemporary culture. Where does most of this knowledge come from today? What sources of evidence are usually provided? Why do we prioritise certain forms of knowledge over others?

Cultural relativism?

Relativists claim that knowledge must be framed within cultural contexts. Knowledge is constructed, maintained and evaluated within culture. The truth or otherwise of a proposition is dependent on the cultural settings it exists in. In its strongest form, cultural relativism insists that there is nothing objective (outside of a particular culture) from which to measure the veracity or otherwise of any statement. In a milder and more convincing form, relativism suggests that knowledge exists in culture and, therefore, different cultures will possess different forms of knowledge. Nevertheless, cultures can point to evidence to substantiate their knowledge claims, and some of these evidences are more compelling than others. In this weaker form, arguments between cultures do not consist of meaningless utterances of taste and preference.

For example, in Britain there is a growing consensus (at least among policy makers) that structured and systematic strategies and assessments, including the use of synthetic phonics, are the most effective way of developing children's language skills. Conversely, countries such as Finland have implemented far more *ad hoc* systems, where children are encouraged to develop these skills through play and communication in less formal systems. As a consequence, English children are heavily 'schooled', while Finnish children spend less time in a school setting than those from any other European country. English 'experts' would point to the success of recent initiatives in improving SAT (Standard Attainment Test) scores, as well as research showing the damaging effects of missed schooling, due to truancy. Finnish 'experts' would point to their continued success at the very top of the PISA (Programme for International Student Assessment) results for literacy, numeracy and science.

Despite clear cultural differences, many philosophers still adhere to a realist position, claiming that apparent cultural differences obscure a great deal of congruence between cultures. For instance, Evers highlights similarities across cultures in 'cognitive scaffolding', including capacities to reason and to think critically, that signal a degree of universality and objectivity (Evers, 2006). From a more objectivist position, there may be obvious differences in the types of knowledge that different cultures value, but some are closer to an objective reality than others. Scientific enquiry may be tentative and fluid, but it is continually moving towards a more coherent and systematic understanding of reality.

Scepticism in an 'information age'

The form that knowledge most commonly takes in contemporary culture is information. Such has been the proliferation of information in the modern Western world that it is frequently referred to as the 'information age'.

Developments in information and communication technology have been profoundly influential in ushering in this new age. Lankshear *et al.* (2000) convincingly articulate how digitisation has reshaped knowledge today. Among other things, they argue that the multimedia digital world results in:

- knowledge that is 'multimodal': by combining text, picture and sound, knowledge takes numerous different forms;
- . . . *rhetorical and normative modes of knowledge* displacing *scientific-propositional on a major scale* (page 35);
- a shift from *propositional knowledge of what already exists* to *knowing as an ability to perform* (page 36).

The effect is a culture saturated with information: where the value of information is judged by how useful it is and how effectively it is presented. As a result, knowledge appears to be increasingly open to contestation: a source of disagreement, argument and speculation. 'Postmodernists' inform us that knowledge:

. . . is more ambiguous and unstable than we had previously thought. It refers to proba-bilities rather than certainties . . . and it is constantly changing as each individual or group gives a particular interpretation to it, reflecting different needs and experiences.

Beck, 1993, page 6

The idea that absolute certainty is unobtainable is not new. A group of philosophers in ancient Greece, known as the 'sceptics', tried to doubt absolutely everything. This position has become known as 'global scepticism': we cannot really know anything. Everything we call knowledge is, in fact, mere opinion. From this perspective, knowledge comprises the opinions of the people we choose to listen to, the ones with the most persuasive arguing techniques or the greatest access to mass communication systems. For the global sceptic, we should believe nothing absolutely and trust nobody.

What is new is that this sceptical outlook seems to have become *normalised* within contemporary culture. This is fallacious and dangerous. As popular opinion of science is contaminated by this sceptical mindset, a partial and mistaken perspective has emerged, that discounts the advantages of basing knowledge on reliable evidence, attempted objectivity, rational enquiry, the search for knowledge and progress. Moreover, if trust in knowledge is abandoned, then the following questions are raised regarding education: What should be part of the curriculum? Why should students put the effort into learning things that are not true? Why should they listen to teachers? What and how should teachers teach?

The benefits of a sceptical outlook

Nevertheless, a sceptical outlook importantly shapes educational processes within contemporary culture. Today, learning is conceived as involving more than the acquisition of knowledge. As they move through education, young people are encouraged (and then expected) to interpret and evaluate established knowledge. More than previously, subject knowledge is open to discussion and challenge. Learning entails developing the capacity to think critically and to question established theories and perspectives.

A sceptical outlook enhances learning in the following ways:

* *as a device to clarify the foundations of knowledge*: as Descartes famously discovered in his 'Meditations' (2008), doubt enables the learner to appreciate what makes knowledge trustworthy;
* *by identifying hidden suppositions*: it helps the learner to uncover the preconceptions and assumptions on which knowledge is built;
* *by ascertaining more dependable knowledge*: the knowledge that survives a sceptical outlook is likely to be more secure and reliable;
* *by encouraging a critical approach*: the learner actively engages with knowledge. Rather than passively accepting knowledge, the learner is in a position to question. To use Postman and Weingartner's phrase, they learn how to be better *crap-detectors* (1971);
* *as a check on prejudices and passions*: it encourages the learner to detach from, reflect on and challenge their beliefs and values (and the ways that these values and beliefs frame their comprehension of knowledge);
* *by promoting the consideration of alternatives*: conceiving of knowledge as flexible rather than inert enables the learner to explore and experiment rather than adhere to static 'truths'.

Of course, this might all seem rather idealistic. This approach to learning and teaching clearly sits more comfortably within certain disciplines. It is harder to conceive of learning experiences like this in the mathematics or science class for instance. But it is certainly not impossible. Perhaps more problematic is the perspective of the learner who feels threatened, inhibited or frustrated by the lack of certainty (no definitive right and wrong answer). A sceptical outlook can make the learner feel exposed and vulnerable, and the teacher today needs to recognise and respond to this. A lack of absolute certainty can be just as aggravating to the learner as fixed and restrictive truths can be.

Pragmatism and 'do-it-yourself' knowledge?

In the early part of the twentieth century, one of the most influential educational philosophers, John Dewey, articulated a theory called pragmatism that consisted of the following features (Hickman and Alexander, 1998):

- *knowledge refers to what is useful*: truth means what is good for the public and for individuals at a particular time;
- *focus on practical and everyday living*: the concentration of knowledge makers should be for the benefit of society, especially in aiding the development of a democratic community;
- *common experience*: knowledge must be built on everyday experience and not on an abstract or metaphysical level;
- *truth is an instrument*: knowledge should be used by people to solve problems and to make sense of situations;
- *cultivation of social experimentation*: avoiding absolute knowledge results in an exploratory climate which is continually evolving and discovering new relevant truths;
- *as situations change, truth changes*: knowledge must be conceptualised as fluid and progressive rather than fixed and restrictive.

From a pragmatic perspective, teaching is not concerned with transmitting a body of existing static information, it is concerned with creating worthwhile learning experiences: most importantly, that stimulate the desire to continue learning (Mason, 2000, page 346). And this seems especially appropriate within the current cultural contexts. Fluidity, plurality and uncertainty necessitate social actors with the capacity to be flexible and autonomous: to critically engage with existing information and to search for alternatives. Nietzsche coined the term *übermensch* (supermen): social experimenters who exist outside of convention and who create knowledge. He viewed freedom from the constraints of existing knowledge as life-affirming (1998). Today, digital tools offer learners the chance to participate in the generation and presentation of information: through activities such as social networking, blogging, podcasting and wiki. There are increasing, albeit limited, opportunities to become 'DIY knowledge makers', and this has tremendous potential for engaging and empowering learning experiences.

Learning in uncertainty

Yet, the mindset of contemporary culture seems somewhat ambivalent. Simultaneously, we are extremely self-confident in the extent and breadth of our own knowledge and achievements, and fearful of contingency, uncertainty and the things we don't know. For Wain (2006), this fearfulness fills us with a need for reassurance and this considerably shapes educational settings:

. . . our obsession with management and transparency is a fear of the uncertain . . . Performativity is the postmodern myth of hope and reassurance, of progress in our world.

Wain, 2006, pages 38–9

Teachers and learners seek the reassurance of measurable outcomes and performance indicators, externalised curriculum and assessment and definitive right and wrong answers to legitimate and anchor their actions. But they also seek the freedom to think independently and creatively, to offer their own insights and interpretations, to be able to take chances and to develop new ideas.

Learning must accommodate the complexity of knowledge within contemporary culture: children and young people need to be taught solid foundations (like scientific and mathematical knowledge) as well as the capacities to think critically, autonomously and creatively. Both are essential to successful learning. Mason offers a useful depiction of the teacher within contemporary culture as *critical mediators of knowledge* (2000). As socio-cultural critics, he argues, teachers must be cultural 'conservers' and 'subversives', both supporting and challenging conventional ways of thinking. The role occupies a middle ground between transmitter of knowledge (as fixed and universally true) and of critical thinking facilitation (presenting knowledge as *provisional and tentative*) (Mason, 2000, page 351).

Practical Task

Think about the forms of knowledge that are most valued on your degree programme. Design and implement a small-scale research project that examines your course. Perhaps you could examine course material and assessment tasks or you could interview some of your peers and gather qualitative data on their experiences.

Try to uncover the following:

- how far does the course presuppose existing 'factual' knowledge?;
- where are there opportunities to participate in DIY knowledge making?;
- how far are you encouraged to approach knowledge with a sceptical outlook?;
- what types of evidence are most/least credible?;
- how do lecturers and students feel about constructions of knowledge?

Learning about morality

Alongside conserving and assessing knowledge, education is concerned with the transmission and acquisition of appropriate or 'good' behaviour. Through it, children and young people are socialised into the norms and values of their culture. So teaching involves shaping and changing people. Moreover, learning and teaching are interactive and relational activities and are, as such, essentially embedded in moral choices and judgements. Education provides an early opportunity for children to mix with others outside their close family. The lessons they learn in school will impact considerably on who they become. For many educational philosophers, therefore, teaching is essentially a moral activity (Buzzelli and Johnston, 2002).

A moral reality?

For much of the last two millennia, Western culture has been dominated by religion. Due to their closeness to God, religious leaders had significant authority. This was consolidated by the fact that these religious leaders were literate, while the 'masses' were not. As messengers of God, they were sole presenters and arbiters of moral truth. The culture that results from this type of arrangement is often referred to as 'moral realism'. From this perspective:

- there are objective moral truths;
- morality exists independently of subjective opinions or feelings;

- different cultures may hold different values but these are right or wrong in themselves;
- there is extensive moral *convergence* between cultures.

The perspective of moral realism is certainly attractive. Without any recourse to a moral reality, it is difficult to claim one type of behaviour is any better or worse than any other. Actions normally considered intrinsically wrong (like murder, adultery, stealing and violence) become simply matters of cultural taste.

Moral relativism and nihilism

The difficulty for the moral realist is that contemporary culture presents us with a morality that is totally at odds with absolutism. There are multiple ways of living in contemporary culture. Various religions prescribe disparate sets of values. Atheists and agnostics adhere to altogether different foundations for morality. Morality itself has become fragmented, pluralised, fluid, complex and uncertain: it seems too much a matter of contestation, too changeable and sectional, for there to be one set of moral truths.

The idea that there is no moral reality is often referred to as moral relativism. From this perspective:

- there are no moral truths;
- all moral claims are based on subjective judgements;
- values are based on the specific values of one's culture;
- moral statements are actually statements of taste;
- e.g. *Murder is wrong* actually means *I don't like murder.*

Nietzsche feared that the *God is dead* (2001, page 109), by which he meant a decline in the cultural significance of religious conviction. He feared this would result in *nihilism*. While Nietzsche was no fan of religion, especially Christianity which he felt was responsible for making people weak and small, he worried that the majority of people needed something to believe in, to give them guidance and a sense of direction. Without religion, the world might seem empty, without meaning or purpose. This can, Nietzsche thought, lead to a sense of despair at the pointlessness of existence.

Morality today is certainly fractured and contested, but this does not make moral questions meaningless. If we accept the relativists' argument that morality is only meaningful within its cultural contexts, then contexts that are fragmented, plural and fluid result in similar constructions of morality. It is more accurate to conceive of contemporary culture as constituted by multiple and divergent 'enclaves of morality', rather than nihilistic. Today, people need to make moral choices rather than act according to defined moral prescripts. With this complexity, people need guidance in steering a course through today's 'moral maze'.

Moral education in contemporary culture

Evidently, education must play a key role in nurturing the development of moral qualities in the young. But the relationship between morality and education is far from straightforward. A number of contemporary issues make this relationship complex and problematic.

- *A non-moral language of education*: the chief concerns of education today can seem rather removed from morality. Competition, training, vocationalism, business, productivity and performance indicators all place an emphasis on the relationship between education and employment rather than morality. Grading and competition (between pupils, teacher and schools) reinforce an individualist culture that is incompatible with moral thinking.
- *Faith schooling*: within multicultural Britain, many parents and communities want to bring their young up within their own traditions and customs. While this can reinforce the moral

codes of particular cultures, it can be divisive and add to the sense that morality only exists within one's own culture.

- *Curriculum controversies*: a national curriculum which is content heavy and divided into specific subjects might offer little opportunity for moral education. Over-assessment can squeeze anything other than exam-preparation activities. Moreover, subjects specifically designed to address moral issues (such as sex and relationship education and citizenship) frequently have their relevance and rigour questioned.

- *Youth and disaffection*: public voices decry the state of the 'youth of today', who are often viewed and portrayed as irresponsible, undisciplined and alienated. Many young people attach little value to education. Persistent truanting and NEETS ('not currently engaged in employment, education or training') can result in social exclusion. The Conservative shadow minister Chris Grayling recently referred to the *Jeremy Kyle generation* of young men who are outside of society.

- *The authority of education/educators*: Related to the last point, the capacity for teachers to act as positive moral role models has been undermined. In a culture epitomised by *blame*, poor teaching is often perceived as a major cause of social breakdown and indiscipline. Stories of 'sink schools' and 'demoralised teachers' who 'can't control their class' further undermine this authority.

- *A culture of 'moral panic' and a proliferation of 'moral guardians'*: contemporary culture exaggerates and, consequently, distorts fear. Media construct 'folk devils' (from paedophiles to joy riders to muggers). We are told who to fear in simplistic and sensational ways. In a climate like this, serious consideration and discussion of moral complexity is very difficult.

Learning shared values

Teachers inculcate children with the standards that we, as a shared culture, value. This takes place explicitly (through lessons on different cultures or on relationships) and, more importantly, implicitly (through group work activities, teacher–pupil relations) – what is referred to as the 'hidden curriculum'. But, as we have seen, contemporary culture is plural and diverse. A multicultural society entails a multiplicity of values and value systems. Despite this, it might be possible to identify common values that teachers can confidently espouse. Certainly, it seems straightforward enough to identify *immoral* educational values that we can generally agree on. For instance, encouraging learning through the infliction of physical pain is wrong – since corporal punishment was outlawed in 1985. Likewise, condemnation of indoctrination and mental torture (ridicule and abuse of power) seems relatively uncontroversial – although both activities are still likely to take place on occasion.

But are there positive values that are shared in contemporary culture? What values enable diversity and fluidity to flourish? What are the values we would associate with a 'moral person' today? Haydon convincingly states that the chief value teachers must promote within plurality is *an attitude of respect towards human cultural contexts in all their variety* (Haydon, 2006, page 469). Perhaps a more extensive list of values could be drawn up. It might look something like this:

- tolerance;
- empathy;
- understanding;
- responsibility;
- care;

- trust;
- inclusion;
- altruism;
- co-operation;
- honesty.

Reflective Task

Despite the multicultural composition of contemporary Britain, many think it is still plausible to refer to values that are common throughout society. For instance, the Qualifications and Curriculum Authority (QCA) provides a statement of values which can be found on its website (**www.qca.org.uk/**).

Schools and teachers can have confidence that there is general agreement in society upon these values. They can therefore expect the support and encouragement of society if they base their teaching and the school ethos on these values (National Curriculum Online, 2008, page 1).

The QCA group these values into the following categories:

- the self;
- relationships;
- society;
- the environment.

Before looking at the document, try to come up with five value statements you could put under each of these four headings. Remember, these need to be shared throughout contemporary British culture.

Now read through the document. Do you agree that all these values are shared and pertinent? Try to offer and justify additional/alternative values. Finally, choose one value and reflect on strategies you might develop to incorporate it into your teaching.

Moral intelligence

So, the loss of an absolute moral reality does not entail the demise of the significance of morality. Indeed, to some extent, moral questions attain greater value and relevance to daily life. Without absolute external duties to follow, individuals must reflexively engage with their own individual moral judgements and choices. A moral life develops internally, through the dialogue between cultural contexts, interpersonal relations and personal agency, rather than through adherence to fixed duties or constraints (Haste and Abrahams, 2008). To make choices successfully, children and young people need to develop a 'moral intelligence':

'Moral intelligence' is not acquired only by memorization of rules and regulations . . . We grow morally as a consequence of learning how to be with others, how to behave in this world, a learning prompted by taking to heart what we have seen and heard.

Coles, 1997, page 5

A 'moral intelligence' enables people to consider the impacts of their actions, to interact positively with one another, and to channel the knowledge they acquire in socially positive ways. The 'hidden curriculum' is particularly significant in the development of 'moral intelligence'. Implicit school factors encourage children and young people to learn it, including:

- the ethos of the school;
- relationships between teachers and pupils;
- opportunities and spaces for pupils to interact with each other;
- chances to experience diversity in positive ways;

- the organisation of the school, including disciplinary procedures;
- the structure of the classroom;
- approaches to teaching and curriculum;
- teachers' use of language, examples and experiences;
- recreational and social activities.

Practical Task

The following poem makes a compelling case for the moral significance of education:

I am a survivor of a concentration camp.
My eyes saw what no man should witness:
Gas chambers built by learned engineers,
children poisoned by educated physicians,
infants killed by trained nurses.
Women and babies shot and buried by high
school and college graduates.
So, I am suspicious of education.
My request is: Help your students become human.
Your efforts should never produce learned monsters, skilled psychopaths, educated
Eichmanns.
Reading, writing, and arithmetic are important only if they serve to make our children more
humane. (Holocaust Museum, in Pring, 2005, page 24)

In your group, devise and act out a role play between a teacher and a group of learners. In it, try to illustrate an encounter in which the teacher successfully helps her 'students become more human'. Now discuss how far you think all teaching can/should be informed by such moral sensitivity? Should the fostering of a 'humane culture' be the priority at all levels of schooling?

From this perspective, the plurality and uncertainty of contemporary culture offers opportunities rather than threats to morality. Greater access to a wide range of values encourages young people to reflect critically on their existing values and to consider alternatives. The *task of moral education is to teach pupils to handle the plurality of our society in an autonomous way* (Wardekker, 2001, page 103). The 'morally intelligent' person can contribute to the maintenance of existing values as well as to changing them and to developing new ones. Possessing the self-confidence and autonomy, alongside the capacities to reflect critically on existing beliefs and practices and to be open to alternatives, are the requisite qualities for living in uncertainty. This applies equally to questions of knowledge and of morality. And the development of such qualities is reliant on democratic schooling practices.

Teacher–learner relations

Like knowledge and morality, voices of authority are more open to criticism and contestation, as contemporary culture becomes increasingly pluralised, fragmented, uncertain, fluid and complex. There has been a shift from *authority-based* to *negotiation-based relations* (Wardekker, 2001, page 102) and this inevitably impacts on the relationships between teachers and learners. At a most general level, this derives from challenges to universalism, to certainty and to truth. Moral panics surrounding the *collapse of adult authority* within contemporary culture may reflect reactionary conservatism, guilty of overstating and oversimplifying current trends, but they do indicate a growing opposition among young people towards adult institutions. In essence, the ascribed hierarchies of previous generations have become increasingly open to challenge.

The authority of the lecturer

Educators' voices, as the guardians and conveyers of legitimate knowledge, are no longer taken for granted. Both their role and even the knowledge they teach are disputed and opened up to competition from a range of alternative sources of knowledge production: in particular from the opinion leaders of the journalistic media and the greater access to knowledge via the internet. To oversimplify, they go from being *the* authority in a particular field to being one voice in the pluralised and fast-moving *knowledge marketplace*. Bauman (2001) provides a thought-provoking account of the university lecturer's response to this challenge. He argues that the academic either *play(s) the game* (page 135) by measuring their success in business and financial terms or they *withdraw* into *impervious theory, esoteric language* and *social irrelevance* (page 136). Yet, for Bauman, these responses involve submission of intellectual authority. In order to survive and maintain integrity, he argues, universities must embrace uncertainty, fluidity and plurality.

Today's learners are less inhibited by status and more equipped with the skills to complain. Consumerist culture, with its associated rights, has provided them with more access to knowledge and more ability to articulate their interests. Furthermore, children, young people and parents have more opportunities to become 'an authority'. Mass communication and other technological advances have made knowledge far more open and accessible. The internet, in particular, has enabled children and young people to access the 'adult world', wider perspectives and knowledge, as well as to articulate, communicate and share their ideas and experiences with their peers: see the website 'ratemyteachers.com' (**http://uk.ratemyteachers.com/**) for an example of a consumerist mentality in education. Within these emergent cultures the claim of educators to be *the* sole authority is no longer credible. They remain 'an authority', but one of a number of competing voices *with* authority.

These changes place the teacher in a position of ambiguity and tension. Contemporary culture is not an entirely distinctive creature from its predecessors: there has been a change in emphasis rather than a substitution. Society (including policy makers, parents and children) still expects teachers to teach knowledge and shared values, and it is still assumed that teachers should possess authority. In fact, a content-heavy curriculum makes it difficult to do much more than transfer knowledge. Yet a 'jug-and-mug' approach to pedagogy (where the teachers transfer their 'expert' knowledge to their class) can appear anachronistic in contemporary culture. It seems at odds with the interests and experiences of young people and the skills they will require to inhabit plurality, diversity and fluidity.

Critical Thinking Task |

Many educationalists and social commentators claim that the authority of the teacher has become increasingly undermined within contemporary culture. Assess this perspective.

Using newspaper and internet sources, try to provide evidence for and against this challenge to teachers' authority. Compile a list of case studies that demonstrate the range of ways that teachers' authority is questioned or challenged.

How far is it true that teachers' authority is being contested at all levels of education? You might, for example, think that younger children do not have the skills or confidence to challenge their teachers' authority, or that this challenge is more likely to come from their parents or from formal education systems. Consider the following environments:

- pre-school education;
- primary schooling;
- secondary schooling;
- colleges;
- universities.

Finally, assess the threats, challenges and opportunities that changes in authority within classroom cultures result in.

Democracy and deliberation

Many would see an erosion in the authority of the teacher as no bad thing: especially in a culture characterised by knowledge/moral plurality. Rather, they would argue that a schooling system that cultivates active and engaged minds is a prerequisite for a healthy and progressive society. Dewey (1997) conceived of schools as embryonic or mini societies. He argued that a 'progressive' democratic society requires a system of education that emphasises democratic experiences. Through this, children can emulate the skills and dispositions that they are expected to possess as adults. Schools need to provide opportunities for learners to find shared interests through interaction with each other within the classroom: and this is equally important and achievable in primary schools as it is in universities (Acton, 1989).

The tendency within democracy, however, is for each individual to act according to her/his own personal self-interest. This is not what Dewey intended. An alternative to this *rational-choice* model of democracy was proposed by Jurgen Habermas (1981). *Deliberative democracy* has the following basic tenets:

- *communication*: public discussion where individual interests are sublimated in favour of the common good;
- *empathetic reasoning*: each participant must put themselves in the position of other participants to empathise with their perspectives;
- *'ideal speech'*: everyone can participate equally and dialogue is not constrained or distorted;
- *open-minded dialogue*: where there is the possibility that participants can be persuaded to change their minds;
- *reasoned agreement*: ultimately decisions are reached collectively and based on consensus.

We have all been involved in arguments where both parties become increasingly vehement in defence of their position. These arguments disintegrate into shouting matches, where rational discussion towards shared goals seems a long way away. Rather, while one person speaks, the other thinks of more ingenious ways to articulate their own position, or they do not allow the other person the opportunity to speak at all. The process becomes about winning (through clever ridicule and sophistry). The result is almost always further entrenchment into original positions. Habermas has something very different in mind. He conceives of an ideal form of discussion, based on mutual trust and respect, where participants are willing to listen and to risk their original positions. In this form of democratic dialogue, shared goals are examined and new possibilities explored.

The benefits of a deliberative democratic approach to education within uncertainty include the following:

- it encourages learners to adopt an 'enlarged mentality': the priorities of the community override individual preferences;
- in response to objections from others, learners need to develop the capacities to build and sustain convincing arguments;
- learners are not afraid to join the discussions for fear of ridicule;
- it helps to build a sense of togetherness or community, as learners look to build commonalities rather than reinforce differences;
- increased fairness: everyone affected can speak and can say whatever they like;
- positive consequences: all views are equally heard and weighed up against one another so that the most favorable outcomes are achieved;
- it diminishes the role of the teacher as 'expert' and encourages the notion of teachers and pupils learning together.

Education is the key institution to order, shape and progress community and democracy. Through employing democratic principles to learning and teaching, education can prepare children and young people to be active and engaged members of society. This is especially true in a culture that is continually changing and evolving. A progressive democracy, in which knowledge and morality are continuously questioned and redefined, depends on citizens who are articulate, intelligent and rational and who can be relied on to reflect, communicate and participate actively.

In contemporary culture, Giroux has convincingly reclassified teachers as *transformative intellectuals*, with the task of developing critical, hopeful and engaged young people. By creating and nurturing conditions of democratic and critical engagement, dialogue and experimentation, teachers can encourage students to gain both self- and social empowerment (Giroux, 1989, page 102). As Giroux puts it:

Education . . . assigns critical meaning to action, connects understanding with engagement, and links engagement with the hope of democratic transformation . . . it is a precondition for producing subjects capable of making their own histories within diverse economies of power and politics.

Giroux, 2004, page 138

Student voice

Currently, the use of the term 'student voice' has become commonplace to define practices that encourage learner participation. 'Student voice' refers to strategies employed within education to enable children and young people to participate in the organisation of the school, the curriculum, the assessment, the lesson and so on. It can exist on a macro level in national movements and organisations (such as consultation on curriculum design) right down to the micro settings of the classroom (where a teacher might include their pupils in designing medium-term plans or assessment tasks). It can be run entirely by the students (like Student Unions in colleges or universities or the English Secondary Students' Association), with the support of teachers (like student councils or student representatives on school bodies), or by teachers who gather information about the experiences of pupils and students that can be used to shape future practices (through module feedback or student surveys). At their best, 'student voice' strategies cultivate honest dialogue between teachers, policy makers and young people that are used to make real and significant changes.

The two leading academic proponents of 'student voice' in the UK in recent years have been Michael Fielding and Jean Rudduck. Rudduck's research has persuasively shown that:

- *current educational practices underestimate children and young people's social maturity*: the ways that schools are organised and the expectations of those that work with them, undervalue the role children and young people can play;
- *children and young people can contribute positively*: with encouragement and well-thought-out structures, they can play a significant part in the organisation and day-to-day running of the school;
- *students gain from being included in decision making*: consultation and involvement in decision making can impact positively on academic, social and personal development;
- *the 'perils of popularity'*: there are dangers in the current preoccupation with 'student voice' in its existing form. Successful practice must include involvement in meaningful decision making (Rudduck and Fielding, 2006).

Rudduck was particularly concerned that inconvenient and silent voices are all too often marginalised by today's practices. Schools and teachers can engage in 'student voice' practices in a somewhat half-hearted or tokenistic manner. For example, Newman *et al.* (2008) have highlighted concerns that universities are engaged in disingenuous and manipulative activities with the National Student Survey, treating it as a marketing tool rather than a means for students to express their true perspectives.

From his 'Students as Researchers' work (2001), Fielding devised a series of questions intended to assess the conditions for student voice. As the table below demonstrates, effective 'voice' depends on more than the capacity to express oneself. Among other things, it depends on who is listening, how far students are encouraged and trained to participate effectively, and what results from any student–staff dialogue.

Critical Thinking Task

There is a wide variety of student voice strategies in existence today. In a small group, evaluate the effectiveness of a few of these.

Look at the Table 3.1 based on Fielding's framework (2001). Identify student voice strategies in your place of study (it might be module evaluations, student representatives or involvement in writing learning materials/assessments). Try to answer all of the questions. How could the strategies you have chosen be improved?

Table 3.1 Student voice (adapted from Fielding, 2001, page 110)

Domain	Key questions	Your responses
Speaking	Who speaks, to whom, what about?	
Listening	Who listens? Why? How?	
Skills	Is there any training?	
Attitudes and dispositions	Equal/reciprocal relationships?	
Organisational culture	Centrality of student voice in daily practices?	
Spaces	Where does it take place?	
Action	What happens?	
The future	What next? Improvements?	

Now, using the same table, evaluate existing national programmes intended to promote student voice. For instance, take a look at the following:

* English Secondary Students' Association;
* Consulting Pupils about Teaching and Learning project;
* 11million.org.uk (**www.11million.org.uk**): an organisation led by the Children's Commissioner;
* National Student Survey.

Chapter Summary

After reading this chapter, you should recognise that:

* Contemporary culture compels us to rethink traditional approaches to learning and teaching.
* Uncertainty, plurality, fragmentation, complexity and fluidity necessitate distinctive conceptualisations of knowledge, morality and teacher–pupil relations.
* With the current speed of change, information can become rapidly obsolete, and the variety of competing claims in existence today means that learning must involve more than the acquisition of knowledge.
* There are few, if any, moral absolutes for one to learn by rote, and any that might exist are far more contested and problematised than in previous times. In contemporary culture, there is a need for learners to develop a 'moral intelligence'.
* What was a taken-for-granted authority of the teacher is now more open to question and challenge, and this provides both threats and opportunities for the learner.

Research focus

Background

The cultural shifts that this chapter explores are often assumed to characterise a distinctive period termed 'postmodernism'. But this term is far from straightforward. And the relationship between 'postmodern' culture and learning is even more problematic. The following article by Clive Beck examines many of the key contentions of 'postmodernists' and discusses the implications for teaching and learning. How far do you agree with Beck's analysis? Has cultural change continued in the directions Beck outlines?

* Beck, C (1993) Postmodernism, pedagogy, and philosophy of education. *Philosophy of Education*, **www.ed.uiuc.edu/eps/PES-Yearbook/93_docs/BECK.HTM**

Changing contexts for learning and teaching

Read the following two articles – the first one is quite demanding but stick with it as it raises important questions. Lankshear *et al.* consider the impact of digitisation on knowledge and on learning, and Mason looks at the position of teachers in a culture which requires them to be more than 'transmitters of knowledge'. Do these accounts overstate the extent that the construction and presentation of knowledge has changed? How far do you recognise these conditions in your own learning experiences?

- Lankshear, C, Peters, M and Knobel, M (2000) Information, knowledge and learning: some issues facing epistemology and education in a digital age. *Journal of Philosophy of Education* 34 (1): 17–39.
- Mason, M (2000) Teachers as critical mediators of knowledge. *Journal of Philosophy of Education*, 34 (2): 343–52.

Beyond 'voice': evaluating student voice strategies

Within the cultural contexts explored during this chapter, there is a growing call to include children and young people in educational decision-making processes. Advocates claim such practices result in social and personal benefits. But the popularity of 'student voice' strategies often conceals superficial adherence on behalf of teacher and schools. Read the following papers and reflect on why giving learners a voice is especially important within contemporary culture, and what forms these strategies might most effectively take.

- Fielding, M (2001) Beyond the rhetoric of student voice: new departures or new constraints in the transformation of 21st century schooling? *Forum*, 43 (2): 100 – 109.
- Fielding, M (2007) Beyond 'voice': new roles, relations, and contexts in researching with young people. *Discourse: Studies in the Cultural Politics of Education*, 28 (3): 301–10.

Chapter 4

Learning to live in uncertainty: perspectives from psychology

Learning outcomes

By the end of this chapter you should be able to:

- briefly outline the most significant cultural theories of learning in psychology (Vygotsky, Bruner, social constructivism);
- utilise notions of 'multiple intelligence', 'emotional intelligence' and 'learning styles' to examine broader conceptualisations of learning today;
- outline and illustrate the significance of culture on child development;
- make use of 'learning to learn' literature to reflect on the characteristics of effective learning in contemporary culture.

Chapter outline

Psychologists have had a particular interest in and influence on learning. In fact, above all of the other disciplines utilised in education studies, psychology has had the greatest impact on our understanding and practices of learning. While teacher training courses are frequently criticised for underplaying the importance of theory, psychological conceptualisations of learning remain relatively commonplace. During the course of their studies, most trainee teachers will encounter the core theories of behaviourism, cognitivism, humanism and constructivism. But detailed examination of learning theory has become the preserve of the Education Studies degree.

Learning is a personal process mediated in the social and cultural contexts of the school, college or university. This chapter concentrates on theories that understand learning in these cultural contexts, rather than those that explain learning as mental activity. Psychologists who have influenced educational thought and practice from this latter perspective, including 'behaviourists' like Pavlov and Skinner and 'cognitivists' like Piaget and Ausubel, are not considered in detail. Nevertheless, while the chapter focuses on cultural contexts, it is important to recognise that the cultural and personal aspects of learning are not mutually exclusive.

A number of cultural theorisations and influences are discussed during the chapter, including:

- linking learning with culture (Vygostsky and Bruner);
- multiple intelligences (Gardner);
- emotional intelligence (Goleman);
- learning styles and individualised learning (Riding and Rayner);
- child development and the importance of play (Moyles);
- *toxic childhood* (Palmer);
- emergence of 'tweenagers' and changing notions of adolescence;
- *learning to learn* and metacognition (Claxton).

A cultural understanding of learning – from 'inside out' to 'outside in'

Some of the contributions of psychology to a culture of learning have been far from positive. For much of the second half of the twentieth century, the prevalent perception of intelligence was of an innate ability inside each individual. Intelligence was understood as something static, straightforward and measurable. Based on the (now largely discredited) work of the psychologist Cyril Burt, generations of children were assigned an intelligence quotient at the age of 11. They were then placed in what was regarded as an appropriate level of schooling for their prescribed ability. While the perspective that intelligence is related to biology and that learning is something that happens inside the individual remains powerful in psychology, an alternative cultural perspective emerged in the 1960s and has grown in strength and importance since then. In fact, the psychological discipline has done most to challenge these straightforward and essentialist conceptions of learning.

The work of the Russian, Lev Vygotsky, and the American, Jerome Bruner, has proved particularly important in doing this. Although Vygotsky died in 1934, his work did not reach a worldwide audience until the 1960s, with some of his work not translated into English until the 1990s. Whereas Piaget was primarily interested in the internal mental processes of cognitive development, Vygotsky emphasised the importance of culture. He argued that human activity takes place within cultural settings, in the social interactions between people, and therefore cannot be understood without reference to these settings. Two of Vygotky's concepts have proved especially significant for our understanding of learning:

- *cultural tools*: just as humans use material tools to develop their physical abilities, they use cultural tools to develop their psychological abilities. Cultural tools include language, symbols, numbers, pictures, models, plans and maps. Education introduces children to these cultural tools, showing them how to use them, so that they can develop positive abilities and personalities. Through the use of the term 'cultural tools', Vygotsky connects psychological development with learning and culture;
- *a zone of proximal development*: Vygotsky distinguished between a child's actual and potential developmental level. Provided they are given appropriate support, a child has the potential to move beyond their current stage of development. During supported and guided conversations and interactions with a more competent member of culture (an older peer or a teacher), the child progresses intellectually. The space between what the learner already knows and what is currently too difficult for them to grasp is what Vygotsky refers to as the 'zone of proximal development'.

Bruner was heavily influenced by Vygotsky's ideas. Vygotsky had introduced important and broad concepts, and Bruner developed and applied these to educational contexts. He was particularly interested in identifying the actual processes and activities that a teacher might use to support a child in achieving goals that would otherwise be beyond their current stage of development. To do this, Bruner introduced a key learning concept:

- *scaffolding*: if learning takes place in this 'zone of proximal development', then the role of the teacher is essential to the learning process. The teacher must structure the child's activity, ensuring that they are neither bored nor lost. A wide range of 'scaffolding' strategies have been developed by Bruner and by others since, including breaking problems down into manageable steps, providing concrete examples and modelling actions. Crucially, the teacher gradually withdraws control and support as the child becomes more competent in a given task. The 'Socratic method' of teaching, evident in Plato's dialogues, may be considered an early example of such 'scaffolding'.

In 1996, Bruner wrote *The Culture of Education*. Early in the book, he distinguishes between culturalism and computationalism in psychology. Whereas computationalists are concerned with the world from the perspective of the internal mind, he argues, culturalists focus on 'the external' and its impact on the mind. While the book does not reject either perspective, it explores culturalism, the process of 'meaning-making', and the implications for education (Bruner, 1997). Two concepts are central:

- *narrative*: Bruner argues that the world consists of stories. Education has a tendency to rely on one such story, based on the enlightenment ideals of objective enquiry, scientific method and progress that you encountered in earlier chapters. For Bruner, teaching ought to explore narrative: the complex, fluid and conflicting interpretations that the social world is made up of. The learning process must prepare children to live in a reality made up of multiple narratives.

We live most of our lives in a world constructed according to the rules and devices of narrative. Surely education could provide richer opportunities than it does for creating the metacognitive sensitivity needed for coping with the world of narrative reality and its competing claims.

Bruner, 1997, page 149

- *intersubjectivity*: broadly speaking, intersubjectivity refers to a two-way communication between people. Rather than existing independently, meaning is constructed in communication: hence the term 'meaning-making'. Bruner is interested in the implications of intersubjectivity for a *pedagogy of mutuality* (1996, page 56). The child should not be viewed as an empty vessel ready to be filled with objective knowledge. Rather, learners and teachers must engage in a process of discussion and collaboration, and in so doing, construct shared meanings of reality together.

Social constructivism and learning

Constructivism is a broad and complex perspective spanning a range of disciplines. Within psychology, Vygotsky is often seen as central to constructivist ways of thinking. His ideas have been updated and applied to Western education by David Wood (1997) who emphasises learning as a social activity, dependent on interactions and cultural contexts. While theorists described as social constructivists would disagree about many things, there are some general values and beliefs that are characteristic of the perspective:

- the learner is an individual, with a unique set of prior cultural experiences;
- learners should increasingly take responsibility for their own learning;
- the teacher should be a facilitator, not an informer – asking questions, not providing answers;
- learning environments should be complex and dynamic, exploring multiple perspectives;
- learning tasks should be relevant;
- the learner should be encouraged to participate in the decision-making process;
- learners should be encouraged to understand their role in the process of knowledge construction: how their values, beliefs and previous experiences shape their perspectives on the world;
- learning is an active and social process, with the learner at the centre;
- a 'community of learners' should be fostered, whereby learners are encouraged to view learning as a shared and co-operative enterprise.

Practical Task

Educators influenced by social constructivist notions of learning have come up with a range of approaches for teachers to utilise. Search for information on the following six teaching and learning strategies: you might use the indicative references to get you started. Write a short paragraph outlining the main characteristics for each:

- learning communities (see Bielaczyc and Collins, 1999);
- enquiry learning (see Hutchings, 2006);
- learning by teaching (see Goodlad and Hirst, 1989);
- problem-based learning (see Schwartz, 2001);
- instructional conversation (see Goldenberg, 1991);
- guided participation (see Rogoff *et al.*, 1993).

Select the strategy that you are most convinced by. Using your chosen strategy, undertake a short piece of action research (whereby you develop a lesson plan, then trial, evaluate and redesign it).

The Teaching and Learning Research Programme (TRLP) is a key UK research initiative aimed at improving outcomes for learners at all stages of education. It recently proposed *10 principles for effective teaching and learning* (TRLP, 2007). Have a look at these principles and consider the extent that they correspond with social constructivist perspectives? Can you suggest an alternative principle that would fit more appropriately?

In *Teaching as a Subversive Activity* (1971), Postman and Weingartner outlined a highly influential method of teaching based on the social constructivist approach. They termed it the *inquiry method* and it consisted, among other things, of the following:

- not telling students what they 'ought to know';
- lessons developing according to students' responses (not pre-planned structure);
- avoiding giving summaries;
- avoiding making evaluations about student contributions;
- each lesson posing problems for students;
- encouraging student-to-student rather than teacher-to-student interaction;
- successful teaching entails facilitating 'good student' characteristics, (such as self-confidence; confidence in own judgement; flexibility; not afraid of being wrong; enjoying problem solving; being at ease with a lack of straightforward answers).

If anything, strategies like 'inquiry method' are more appropriate today then when Postman and Weingartner devised it. Certain aspects of contemporary culture have become so fast-paced, complicated and multiple; the speed at which things change is so great that it is difficult to make predictions or to plan out coherent life and career trajectories. Information seems increasingly open to contestation, seemingly contradicted and updated daily. Many social arrangements have become fragmented and divergent: people live very different lives from one another, drawing from an ever-growing number of lifestyle choices.

Within these settings, individuals need to possess the personal qualities and skills to cope with (and even embrace) complex and fractured life courses. Young people must leave school able to engage with problems, to come up with their own solutions, and to respond to their ever-changing circumstances. It is difficult to say how far formal schooling has gone in recognising this. In all likelihood, there is far more good practice than critics would want us to believe.

There are also still plenty of young people whose primary experience of schooling involves copying down and memorising a list of 'facts' from a whiteboard.

Learning and culture

Psychological theory has considerably shaped our understanding of learning within contemporary culture. Four cultural facets of learning have proved particularly significant:

- teacher–pupil relations and classroom culture;
- learning and intelligence;
- learning styles;
- the significance of play.

Teacher–pupil relations and classroom culture

Alongside sociologists, social psychologists have repeatedly demonstrated the importance of classroom encounters on learning: most notably in Rosenthal and Jacobsen's infamous experiment of 1967 (Rosenthal and Jacobsen, 2003). Crucial learning concepts such as 'labelling', 'typing' and 'self-fulfilling prophecy' have been developed. Sociologists have been preoccupied with exploring how these micro-level encounters help to construct and reproduce class, gender and ethnic inequalities. Social psychologists have been concerned with investigating the impact of these interactions on the self-identity of learners.

One of the main early groups to recognise the importance of settings and relations were the humanists, who developed a person-centred approach to teaching and learning. Coming to prominence in the 1960s and 1970s, the work of theorists like Rogers and Maslow encouraged educators to think of the learner as a whole person, with particular needs, interests and desires. For instance, Maslow famously highlighted the need for safety, self-esteem and a sense of belonging if a learner is to fulfil their potential (Maslow, 1970). Without security, the pupil will lack the confidence to learn independently.

This clearly focuses attention on the teacher and their ability to foster a safe, warm and nurturing learning culture in their classroom. Another influential humanist psychologist and educator of the time was Haim Ginott. He argued that teachers have a key role in cultivating a positive classroom culture and that this is essential in terms of the qualities that children develop throughout their lives. Among other things, Ginott (1972) argued that *rebellion follows rejection* and that *dependency breeds hostility*.

Reflective Task

The greater the emphasis education places on person-centred learning, rather than knowledge transference, the more significant the qualities of the teacher become. For the famous educator and psychologist, Haim Ginott, this elevates the role of educator to tremendously high levels:

I have come to a frightening conclusion. It is my personal approach that creates the climate. It is my daily mood that makes the weather. As a teacher, I possess tremendous power to make a child's life miserable or joyous. I can be a tool of torture or an instrument of inspiration. I can humiliate or humor [sic], hurt or heal. In all situations it is my response that decides whether a crisis will be escalated or de-escalated, a child humanized or de-humanized.

Ginott, 1972, pages 15–16

Take each line from this famous extract and try to come up with an appropriate personal anecdote: either from your time as a student or during work experience. Do you agree with Ginott that the teacher is fundamentally important to classroom culture and in the development of children as *humanized or de-humanized* people? What types of teacher behaviour are most/least humanising?

More recently, some psychologists have focused on particular changes in the classroom environment and the impact on the culture of learning. One particularly interesting and contemporary study was conducted by Janet Schofield (1995). Schofield was interested in how technology interacts with classroom culture. Her fieldwork explored what happens to learning when computers are introduced into the classroom. She uncovered a number of positive results, including:

- students working on computers meant that the teacher became less of an authority figure;
- students had much more control and freedom over their learning;
- students viewed the teacher as a helper;
- students talked with each other;
- students could take on the role of the 'expert';
- students helped each other;
- students felt confident to experiment more because they had privacy with their computer;
- goals were changed – from reliance on the teacher to overcoming personal challenges (see also Collins and Bielaczyc, 1999).

You might find these results rather surprising. Poorly managed computer-based lessons can result in learners who are isolated, fragmented and confused: the opposite of the humanised democratic and collaborative culture that Schofield describes. Many young people are far from 'experts' in using computers. Technology can be intimidating and can result in learners becoming far more dependent on their teacher and far less experimental. Moreover, the vast amount of information accessible through the internet can be overwhelming. Learners need support in evaluating the merits of different sites and they need direction towards appropriate material. Clearly, digitisation and e-learning provide all sorts of opportunities for learners, but positive learning experiences depend on skilled facilitation.

Learning and intelligence

Another major psychological influence on learning and culture today is our changing understanding of intelligence. As noted above, there has been a shift away from intelligence as a fixed, inherited and single entity, related solely to intellectual achievements. Educators today are more likely to use the word 'attainment' rather than 'ability' and this reflects a shift away from an essentialist and biological understanding of intelligence. Moreover, a wider understanding and use of the word 'intelligence' has emerged.

Howard Gardner has made the most significant contribution to contemporary con-ceptualisations of intelligence, by introducing the notion of 'multiple intelligence' (1999). Gardner argued that it is better to think of many forms of intelligence, with each individual possessing their own unique blend. While closely associated with one another, Gardner distinguished between eight or twelve of these intelligences (Smith, 2008). Cultures place different values on each intelligence, dependent on the skills that are requisite to given times and places. The British education system clearly prioritises linguistic and logical-mathematical intelligences over the more personal and physical forms that Gardner presents.

Among the intelligences Gardner establishes are:

- *linguistic*: to learn and use languages (e.g. essay writer);
- *logical-mathematical*: to analyse problems logically (e.g. problem solver);
- *musical*: to compose, perform and appreciate music (e.g. band member);
- *bodily-kinaesthetic*: movement and hand–eye co-ordination (e.g. footballer);
- *spatial*: to perceive the physical world accurately (e.g. art student);
- *interpersonal*: to understand other people's moods and desires (e.g. friend);
- *intrapersonal*: to understand one's own strengths and weaknesses (e.g. creative writer);
- *naturalistic*: – to use the environment effectively (e.g. school allotment helper);
- *existential*: to contemplate big questions about the meaning of life (e.g. critical thinker).

Gardner's work has been subjected to serious criticism. Academics have challenged the extent that these intelligences are distinct and independent from one another, and whether some of them (including interpersonal) would be better described as talents or personality traits rather than intelligences. Gardner himself criticised the misapplication of his ideas within schools: most particularly the inappropriate grading of intelligences and the use of all intelligences in all lessons (in Woolfolk *et al.*, 2008, page 136). Despite concerted criticism, his work has proved highly influential and popular with teachers and has profoundly influenced educational thinking and practice.

One particular form of intelligence has come to prominence in contemporary culture: 'emotional intelligence'. Popularised by Daniel Goleman (1996), emotional intelligence refers to:

. . . the ability to understand, manage and express the social and emotional aspects of one's life in ways that enable the successful management of life tasks such as learning, forming relationships, solving everyday problems, and adapting to the complex demands of growth and development.

Elias *et al.*, 1997, page 6

Associated with Gardner's notions of intrapersonal and interpersonal, then, emotional intelligence refers to the ability to appreciate feelings (in oneself and in others), to use them effectively and to manage negative emotions: such as anger, fear or depression. Goleman provocatively titled his book *Emotional Intelligence: why it can matter more than IQ* (1996). But he never really pins down what 'emotional intelligence' is and where it comes from, favouring instead to tell a series of stories. It is certainly difficult to accurately measure a persons 'emotional intelligence', how to systematically build it into curriculum, or how to use it to predict how individuals will react in different situations. As with 'multiple intelligence', critics claim theorists like Goleman have conflated two distinctive personal qualities: the capacities to think and to feel.

Although 'multiple' and 'emotional' intelligences are highly controversial theories, they are both indicative of changes in our comprehension of learning in contemporary culture. Both encourage policy-makers and teachers to educate the whole child: to support social and emotional as well as intellectual development.

Learning styles

Arguably the most significant contribution that psychology has made to culture and learning is in the area of learning styles. While learning styles are different from multiple intelligences, the two are frequently associated with one another. Put simply, learning styles are concerned with the different *ways* individuals think, learn and behave, whereas multiple intelligences identify the different *types* of abilities individuals possess. Prominent in the 1950s and 1960s, learning styles went out of fashion for a long period, but re-emerged in the 1990s. This was largely due to the growing emphasis on personalised learning and differentiation: the use of learning styles inventories appeared to enable teacher and learner to recognise the diversity and complexity of learning. Designed to identify and allocate students a particular learning style, inventories seemed to offer an important pedagogic tool and one that could be utilised fairly effortlessly.

Inventories have mass appeal and have also been subjected to extensive critique. Both are in large part due to the wide array of learning styles and personality-types theorisations in existence. Distinctions between learning styles are based on a variety of factors. For instance, Riding and Rayner identify quite specific cognitive skills: individuals' preferred ways of *organising and representing information* (Riding and Rayner, 1998, page 25). On this basis, they distinguish between learners who prefer 'verbal' or 'imagery' and 'wholist' or 'analytic' styles. Alternatively, the famous 'Myers–Briggs type indicator' (MBTI, 2008) refers to broad personality traits, distinguishing ranges of 'introvert–extrovert', 'sensing–intuitive', 'thinking–feeling' and 'perceiving–judging'. Depending on which inventory you use, you will get a very different sense of the kind of learner you are – and there are hundreds of models in circulation. There is certainly something for everyone, though it is difficult to know who has got it right!

Over the last 15 years, learning styles have become widely used in schools. Today, it is common practice for learners to complete an inventory early on in their studies: most commonly, to discover whether they are predominantly 'visual', 'auditory' or 'kinaesthetic' learners. For many, learning styles material helps to inform both teacher and learner that individuals learn in different ways and that this needs to be taken into account, both in classroom interactions and in helping learners to understand their own strengths and limitations.

A comprehensive literature review of 71 learning styles inventories used in post-compulsory education was completed in 2004 (Coffield *et al.*, 2004). The report argued that there is significant 'conceptual confusion' and 'a bedlam of contradictory claims', as well as a lack of self-criticism, reliability and validity in research. Though it argues learning styles can aid pupils (and teachers) in recognising their own strengths and weaknesses, the review states that its present use has negligible impact on teaching and learning.

Sharp *et al.* (2008) ask the question *VAK* (i.e. visual, auditory or kinaesthetic) *or VAK-uous?'* They compellingly demonstrate a real disparity between learning styles research in psychology and education (the 'strong' version) and the ways that VAK is understood and practised in schools today (the 'weak' version). While expressing some reservations about the 'strong' version of learning styles, it is the 'weak' version that is of particular concern to them. The 'weak' version of VAK, they argue, is based on false assumptions and associations, and trivialises the learning process. They conclude that the, *labelling of children in schools as visual, auditory or kinaesthetic learners is not only unforgivable it is potentially damaging. . .* (Sharp *et al.*, 2008, page 311).

The significance of play

In Britain, it would be fair to say that there has been a reluctance to view play as having much developmental significance. Unlike other countries in Europe, Britain has traditionally constructed a fairly clear distinction between work and play. In recent years, though, compelling evidence has shown that play is central to the healthy development of the child. Again, the influence of Vygotsky is evident. He viewed play as the ideal space for children to acquire and test new abilities and skills. For Vygotsky, play allows children to explore new knowledge and ideas through interaction:

A child's greatest achievements are possible in play – achievements which tomorrow will become his average level of real action.

Cited in Karpov, 2006, page 151

Psychologists have shown that play is vital in developing physical, social and emotional, as well as intellectual capacities: the work of Janet Moyles (2005) has been especially important in confirming this. During play, children learn to interact with one another and with adults. They learn to take the roles of others and to begin to see themselves as others see them. They learn how to cope with difficult situations, to manage conflict and to express emotions in socially acceptable ways.

There are many different types of play that children participate in, each helping them learn particular skills:

- *sensorimotor play*: to control and use the body;
- *pretend play*: to learn about roles, norms and customs;
- *language play*: to become more accomplished with language;
- *solitary play*: to be able to occupy oneself;
- *social play*: to interact with others;
- *exercise play*: to develop co-ordination and physical strength;
- *free play*: to become more independent and autonomous;
- *rough-and-tumble play*: to learn how to deal with conflict;
- *socio-dramatic play*: to take on the role of others;
- *thematic fantasy play*: to develop imagination and to cope with fears.

As a result, today the value of play is recognised far more. Government, charities, schools and businesses are marketing play as a learning activity and investing heavily in it. For instance, in 2008 the Rose Review of primary schooling recommended further training in play-based learning for teachers (Rose, 2008, pages 53–4). Arguably, the concern now is not that children play too much, but that the opportunities to play are being eroded.

Practical Task

Today many people express concern about the limited opportunities children have to play. They point to the sell-off of significant amounts of school land, to few open spaces in urban areas and to concerns over the safety of public areas. While this might be largely true, there are a number of recent strategies aimed at highlighting the learning benefits and providing opportunities for play. For instance, have a look at the websites of the following organisations:

- Play England (**www.playengland.org.uk/**);
- All4Kids UK (**www.all4kidsuk.com/**);
- Early Learning Centre (**www.elc.co.uk**);
- Right to Play (**www.righttoplay.org.uk**);
- Literacy Trust website (**www.literacytrust.org.uk**) under the heading 'play'.

Using the material you have gathered from these sites (and any others you find useful) devise an organisation called 'Learning Through Play'. Create a brochure/leaflet/webpage advertising your strategies/facilities and the reasons why parents should send their children to you.

Child development

There is a tendency to think of childhood as a biological reality: defined by the physical and mental abilities of a particular stage of development. Children are in childhood because they are smaller than adults, are unable to function independently, are emotionally and intellectually immature. But this is far too simplistic. Childhood, as distinct from infancy, is a relatively new invention. Aries has convincingly shown that 'childhood' did not exist prior to the seventeenth century, and it certainly would have looked very different 100 years ago (Aries, 1996). Moreover, childhood refers to very different things around the world. In some places, it does not exist in any form that would make sense to us. For instance, think of images in the news of children carrying guns and engaging in war, or the numbers of children around the world who do not attend schools.

As such, childhood is largely socially constructed. It is moulded by culture, to fit the needs and the values of the society it exists within. The status of a child, the activities they participate in and the ones they are excluded from, their appearance, levels of dependence and power are all shaped by their culture. While physical maturation and cognitive development are important, in a very real sense, individual children are the product of the environment they are surrounded by. In childhood, the individual learns (or fails to learn) how to be a successful member of their society. Given this, psychologists have been especially interested in examining the qualities of the culture that children grow up in. A chief concern has been a so-called 'crisis in childhood' and the potential implications on children's mental and social wellbeing.

'Toxic childhood'?

Sue Palmer's *Toxic Childhood* (2006) has proved a popular and provocative book. In it, Palmer argues that contemporary culture has resulted in *toxic childhood syndrome* and that childhood is in need of *detoxification*. She claims that, *every year children become more distractible, impulsive and self-obsessed – less able to learn, to enjoy life, to thrive socially* (Palmer, 2006, page 14). Driven by technological advancement, culture has changed so dramatically and speedily that the damaging side-effects have gone largely unnoticed. Palmer points to a number of factors contributing to this syndrome, including:

• watching too much television;
• couch-potato lifestyle;
• unsafe environments/streets;
• unhealthy junk food;
• irregular sleep patterns;
• constant exposure to advertising and celebrity culture;
• violent media (DVD, computer games);
• exposure to dangerous people through the internet;
• lack of interaction/emotional bonding with parents;
• a school curriculum that is too full;
• teaching strategies that do not enable children to be active/involved;
• fewer playing fields;
• fewer school trips/extra-curricular activities.

While concern about the effects on childhood of these types of changes is nothing new, Palmer makes a compelling and accessible case. She claims that the product of this combination of changes is children who can lack empathy, can be more awkward socially and can have difficulties with learning. An increasingly sedentary lifestyle is certainly bad news for young children. But, while Palmer recognises the kinds of changes she identifies are not entirely negative, perhaps she underplays the new opportunities on offer to children today.

Critical Thinking Task

'Childhood' sounds like a straightforward enough concept, but it is profoundly complex and contested today. It refers to a wide variety of values and practices across different times and locations. It encompasses biological states as well as cultural constructions, such as laws, the activities of leisure, media and fashion industries, beliefs, behaviours and values. It is very difficult to find agreement about when childhood begins and ends, what rights and responsibilities it does and should include, or even whether or not it is a desirable stratum, or stage, in the life-cycle.

In a small group, complete the following tasks:

- write a list of characteristics of childhood today. Share your list with the rest of your group. Now underline all the characteristics that are not defined by biology;
- what, if any, do these characteristics have in common and what does this tell you about constructions of childhood today?;
- can you agree about when and how childhood starts and ends today?;
- discuss the following proposal: *This is the best time ever to be born!* and draw out a table of the advantages and disadvantages of childhood today;
- can you agree as a group about a particular time and place that would have been preferable to be born into?

'Tweenies'?

The terms 'tweenies' and 'tweenagers' have emerged within the last ten years to explain recent cultural changes in pre-teenage childhood cohort. Originally coined to term a marketing demographic, 'tweenagers' are 8- to 12-year-old children who appear to exhibit the characteristics of teenagers more than those of children. The *branding* and *commercial appropriation* (Russell and Tyler, 2002) of childhood, and especially female childhood, has resulted in disturbing trends. The social problems traditionally associated with teenagers (family tensions, educational difficulties, drug and alcohol misuse) are spreading to younger children. The key characteristics of an emergent 'tweenager' age cohort include:

- *educational pressures*: especially national tests, transition from primary to secondary school;
- *'pester power'*: parents with less time to spend with their children and increasing numbers of divorces might be more likely to consent to demands;
- *marketing and consumption patterns*: mobile phones, small versions of teenage clothes (e.g. boob tubes), accessories, jewellery, make up;
- *celebrity culture*: infantilisation of celebrity and especially young females;
- *peer pressure*: to look a certain way, to grow up fast, to try drugs and alcohol.

As with the changes in childhood mentioned in the previous section, these cultural changes provide both opportunities and threats to children and young people. They also must be considered carefully: 'end of childhood' assertions have been around for a long time and frequently make distorted and moralistic claims. It is certainly true that the numbers of 8 to 12 year olds suffering from mental health problems has increased dramatically in recent years. Many would argue that these young people are confronted with stresses and demands that they do not have the experience or skills to cope with. But, on the other hand, this age group has more visibility, more access to information and to means of expression, more commodities targeted at them and more power than this age group will have ever experienced before. In other words, seemingly straightforward claims about changes in contemporary childhood culture (whether these claims are optimistic or pessimistic) risk oversimplifying what are incredibly complex issues.

Learning in uncertainty

Many educationalists have expressed concerns that formal schooling fails to adequately prepare children for the modern world: specifically for a culture of plurality, fluidity and unpredictability. Since the National Curriculum was introduced in 1988, formal education has been content and assessment heavy. This has cultivated young people who are skilled at memorising facts and responding to exam conditions, but who are essentially '*illearnerate*' (Claxton, 2008): reliant on formal educational structures and unable to think autonomously and flexibly.

Reflective Task

A chief concern with formal schooling today is that repeated assessment has inhibited opportunities for 'deep' learning. Young people might leave schooling with an impressive array of qualifications, but the skills they have acquired might not be appropriate to contemporary life. Read this quote from Emily, a 15-year-old GCSE student:

I guess I could call myself smart. I can usually get good grades. Sometimes I worry, though, that I'm just a tape recorder . . . I worry that once I'm out of school and people don't keep handing me information with questions, I'll be lost.

Claxton, 2004, page 1

Claxton describes Emily as *illearnerate*: she has not (and is aware she has not) been taught to learn effectively by school. She knows how to memorise information, but she feels as if she is unable to think autonomously and independently. How far would you claim that your experiences of schooling left you *illearnerate*? Can you think of concrete examples and counter-examples?

The types of teaching and learning practices that produce 'illearnerate' school-leavers might include:

- a preponderance of 'jug-and-mug' teaching – where the teacher transfers her 'expert' knowledge to her class;
- authoritarian teacher–student relations – where the teacher controls class activities tightly, setting and marking all assessment and controlling the learning space;
- content-heavy curriculum – that specifies legitimate knowledge and constrains learning and teaching activity;
- young people learning to be dependent – on teachers' comments, on text book responses, on feedback on their written work;
- rigid and hierarchical school structures – where pupils have little say over what they do;
- school culture and practices that have little in common with wider society.

'Learning to learn'

The phrase *learning to learn* has been around for a long time, but it has become increasingly popular in recent years. It encompasses a range of strategies that encourage the learner to take a central and active role in their learning. Typically, 'learning to learn' incorporates the following ideas:

- *learning is learnable*: it is possible to learn how to learn;
- the emphasis in schools should be on learning rather than teaching;
- by learning how to think, learning can become a lifelong activity: a *learning life* (Claxton, 1999);
- learners need to be encouraged to reflect on their own learning and be able to identify their own strengths and weaknesses;
- effective learning requires motivation and self-confidence and increases self-esteem;
- *learning to learn* is essentially concerned with *metacognition*: the process whereby learners are able to reflect and act on their own learning.

One of the proponents of *learning to learn* today is Guy Claxton (2002, 2006, 2008). While Claxton is especially interested in the brain and its capacity to learn, he is at the forefront in demonstrating the significance of culture in the learning process. His notion of *building learning power* is increasingly viewed as central to effective teaching practice today. Most influentially, Claxton formulated four 'R's of effective learning. *Note that others use different 'R's – for instance, the Campaign for Learning (2008) have five 'R's with only three in common with Claxton.*

A New '4Rs'?

You will be familiar with the '3Rs': reading, 'riting and 'rithmetic. The idea that a core goal of formal education is to produce young people who can read, write and who are numerate is well established and relatively uncontroversial. You might be less familiar with the new '4Rs' (Claxton, 2002).

- *Resilience – being ready, willing and able to lock on to learning*: the capacity to persist when things are not going to plan and to manage distraction effectively.
- *Resourcefulness – being ready, willing and able to learn in different ways*: the capacity to make use of what is available, to ask good questions, to look at things in different ways and to ask for help when appropriate.
- *Reflection – being ready, willing and able to become more strategic about learning*: the capacity to be self-aware and to manage the process of learning effectively.
- *Reciprocity – being ready, willing and able to learn alone and with others*: the capacity to interact in mutually supportive ways with one another, to listen, to be empathetic and to collaborate.

For a full account of Claxton's '4Rs' see *Building learning power* (Claxton, 2002).

The role of the teacher is to nurture (communicate, manage, model) these attributes in learners so that each is able to improve their 'learning power'. Claxton visualises teachers as *learning coaches*, who are there to offer support, encouragement, and motivation. The real activity is undertaken by the learner, who takes responsibility for his own learning.

Claxton has persuasively shown the importance of *building learning power* in contemporary culture. In fact, a common thread through Claxton's recent work is a concern with the unique circumstances of our current way of life. Making use of Kegan's distinction between *automatic* and *stick shift* culture, he argues that the uncertainty of the modern world affords the individual the freedom to invent and reinvent himself, and that this results in both new opportunities and new demands (Claxton, 1999, page 245). Within such a culture, the capacity to learn becomes a prerequisite to a successful life.

Creating a 'learning culture' in the classroom and the school

Claxton argues that learning capacity must be enhanced through an embedded whole-school approach, rather than through particular teaching strategies (in isolation) (Claxton, 2000, 2006). In Britain, he argues, the first steps towards a coherent *learning culture* have been taken:

We are beginning to go beyond the 'hints and tips' approach to discover what type of cultural change, in both individual classrooms, and the school as a whole, is necessary to expand learning capacity. The jumble of mind maps, brain gym, learning styles and multiple intelligences of a few years back was a start – but I think we are now on the track of an approach that is more infused into the fabric of the school, and more intellectually coherent and well grounded.

Claxton, 2006, page 2

And there is plenty of evidence that Claxton is right. Policy makers increasingly use the rhetoric of 'learning to learn' and 'learning power' – and are starting to create more space in the curriculum for learning. Numerous trials based on these ideas are taking place in schools around the country – see Campaign for Learning (2008) for many examples. Academics and professionals decry an educational system that does not allow enough time, space and freedom for 'deep' learning to take place. The idea that 'learning' is concerned with the development of personal, independent qualities rather than the acquisition of 'facts' is certainly becoming more commonplace. If you do an exact-phrase UK Google internet search for *learning to learn* you will come up with around 50 000 entries.

But at present, assessment dominates the culture of learning in Britain. Subject-centred content-heavy curriculum, important summative assessment every few years of a child's schooling, and outcome-based monitoring systems put tremendous pressure on pupils and teachers. In this culture, it is easy to see how 'learning' becomes synonymous with 'preparation for the next exam': the next hurdle to jump. But it is hard to see how this 'learning culture' can be fostered in an educational system that puts such emphasis on assessment.

So can these two cultures of learning co-exist? Probably not! This might be a most significant educational crossroad. The modern world requires citizens (and workers) who are autonomous, who can think independently, who can respond positively to change and unpredictability and who can communicate effectively with one another. Perhaps formal schooling needs to provide the space and freedom for these qualities to be cultivated?

Critical Thinking Task

Is learning how to be an effective learner as important as the traditional skills of literacy and numeracy? Divide yourself into two groups and debate the following proposal:

Learning the 4Rs (resilience, resourcefulness, reflection and reciprocity) is as important for children as the 3Rs (reading, 'riting and 'rithmetic).

Try to reach a position that you can all agree on. You are likely to conclude that learners cannot be effective without core literacy and numeracy skills, but that high-quality education provision must also focus on developing learning proficiency. Read the following inspection advice:

Keep Learning High Profile

Put this on every teacher's desk.

- *What have they learned?*
- *How do you know?*
- *How is this activity helping them learn?*

Put this on every classroom door – so it is the last thing that students will see as they leave the classroom.

- *What have you learned today?*

(from Curtis and Wilcock, 2003, page 11).

What do you think of this idea? After reading this chapter, are there any other questions you would like to add?

Chapter Summary

After reading this chapter, you should recognise that:

- In recent years, there has been a growing movement within psychology to emphasise learning as a cultural enterprise.
- Cultural settings (teacher–pupil relations, classroom and school values and environment) are essentially important to effective learning.
- Psychologists have contributed to a current educational culture that perceives learning as individualised and multiple, as well as socially situated.
- Cultural constructions of childhood and adolescence today offer both threats and opportunities to the learner.
- Teaching strategies that stimulate learners to think independently and interact with one another are most appropriate within contemporary culture – schools must cultivate a learning culture.
- Children and young people must develop metacognitive skills (learn to learn) if they are to develop the capacities necessary to lead successful lives within contemporary culture.

Research focus

Background

The following two sources might be considered seminal works. They should certainly be consulted and included in any learning styles assignments or presentations.

- Coffield, F, Moseley, D, Hall, E and Ecclestone, K (2004) *Should we be using learning styles? What research has to say to practice*. Learning and Skills Research Centre. Trowbridge: Cromwell Press.
- Riding, R and Rayner, S (1998) *Cognitive styles and learning strategies: understanding style differences in learning and behaviour*. London: Fulton.

As you read, pay particular attention to the staggeringly confusing array of models, theoretical frameworks, instruments, applications, interpretations and claims pointing out that learning styles' researchers are certainly not unified in all of their views. Outline what you believe to be the main criticisms of learning styles research presented, highlighting the issues and debates that remain unresolved.

Learning styles and education

While it is commonly asserted that learning styles cannot be ignored in any educational context, there remains considerable disagreement over the perceived status of learning styles as a critical factor in the processes of teaching and learning and how learning styles differences should be addressed in the classroom. The following research report was produced by Demos, an independent think-tank organisation.

- Demos (2004) *About learning: report of the Learning Working Group*. London: Demos.

This report begins to consider how a focus on learning styles is impacting on classroom teaching and learning. Within this report you will find reference to teachers using learning styles in ways that constitute 'poor professional practice'. Identify what the authors mean by 'poor professional practice' and consider the implications of labelling children as visual, auditory or kinaesthetic learners? Why is it important to address a range of learning styles and not simply focus on the one a child might prefer?

VAK

VAK, at least as it is commonly encountered in schools, is not a part of the learning styles 'establishment' where findings are presented and debated at the highest academic level and recorded in peer-reviewed academic journals. Recent forceful critiques of learning styles such as VAK by Franklin (2006) and Sharp *et al.* (2008) have drawn attention to the somewhat casual acceptance and promotion of VAK as conspiring against a teaching profession which prides itself on critical analysis and reflection.

- Franklin, S (2006) VAKing out learning styles – why the notion of 'learning styles' is unhelpful to teachers. *Education*, 3–13: 81–7.
- Sharp, JG, Bowjer, R and Byrne, J (2008) VAK or VAK-uous? Towards the trivialisation of learning and the death of scholarship. *Research Papers in Education*, 23 (3): 293–314.

Read both of these articles carefully. Considering the evidence presented, to what extent do you agree or disagree with these authors? Why do you think VAK is spreading through schools at an alarming rate without proper consideration of the issues and debates involved? How might teachers be more formally directed towards interrogating the underpinning theories, concepts and principles of VAK more deeply, particularly when VAK appears intermingled with such disparate areas as brain-based learning, accelerated learning and multiple intelligences?

Chapter 5

Politics, power and priorities: perspectives on education policy

Learning outcomes

By the end of this chapter you should be able to:

- critically consider governments' involvement in the education provision and opportunities for learning available within society;
- identify competing governmental agendas for education and recognise potential contradictions and tensions that exist between these;
- outline recent trends in policy formation (including networks of governance, new public management and marketisation) and account for their impact on education;
- assess the opportunities offered by recent education policy for the different cultures of learning advocated in previous chapters of this book.

Chapter outline

It should be clear that the manner in which a society constructs and organises learning can have profound influence upon individuals' lives. The competing historical, philosophical and psychological perspectives already presented have shown that there is no single correct set of answers to the questions of what, where, when or how an individual should learn. However, in most contemporary societies these questions are regularly answered by others on our behalf. Most people do not have the opportunity to entirely freely design their own educational pathways: apart from the small percentage of those whose parents have made the decision to educate at home, children in the UK are likely to spend an average of 7 hours a day, 190 days of the year for at least 11 years in formally timetabled, government-regulated schools. Here rules and expectations can be formalised as 'policy' at a number of different levels: in individual classrooms by teachers or heads of department, at a whole-school level by principals and management staff, by local educational authorities and councillors and by national governmental departments and Acts of Parliament. Policymakers can determine *when* an individual learns by setting upper and/or lower age limits on the duration of compulsory education in schools. They can dictate *what* and *how* an individual should learn by establishing a national curriculum and by regulating the pedagogical training that student teachers receive. They can also impact *where* an individual goes to learn by supporting the establishment of different types of educational provision and by helping to determine the selection of students admitted to different schools and colleges each year.

This chapter asks: who exactly is in a position to make formal decisions over what, how, when and where other people learn? What factors and considerations inform or restrict their decision-making process, and what sorts of cultures of learning are constructed as a consequence? It identifies competing governmental agendas for education and draws attention to a number of significant inconsistencies and tensions using case study illustration from recent policy directions taken by the British government.

Policy, politics and government

Most societies acknowledge and accept the need for some form of government authority to provide long-term stability and security. Few human beings live as entirely isolated individuals: most live in interdependent groups and communities, drawing upon each others' skills, strengths and resources to achieve things that would not be possible if everybody acted alone. But the individuals who make up a community still have independent thoughts, opinions and priorities. They may also have conflicting interests and needs. One of the most important roles of government is to arbitrate between competing perspectives and to balance the interests and concerns of individuals with the interests and concerns of the rest of the group. Today, human societies are far too large to be able to involve each individual in every decision-making process. Governments are the institutions that have been given – or have taken – the authority to make and enforce collective decisions on the rest of their society's behalf (Hague and Harrop, 2004). The notion of 'enforcement' is important here: failure to abide by set rules or laws can be punished or sanctioned against.

In Britain, we describe our form of government as a 'democracy': our politicians are voted into office and can be voted out again if they are seen to make too many bad decisions or lose sight of the people whom they are supposed to represent. Different political parties articulate competing visions of what a society should aspire to and how best to reach that goal. Because there is not only one correct template for the 'good society', politics will always be a contested and dynamic domain. For example, one of the issues that individuals and political parties regularly disagree about is exactly how far the influence and authority of government should extend. Are smoking bans in public places, fines for riding in a car without a seatbelt, or high-profile campaigns to eat more fruit and vegetables an appropriate response from concerned government or an attack on individual freedom of choice and liberty? What about compulsory parenting classes for the legal guardians of children who repeatedly misbehave at school?

Reflective Task

The English philosopher Thomas Hobbes (1588–1679) famously wrote that, without any form of government, human life would be *solitary, poor, nasty, brutish and short*. He believed that individuals were inherently selfish and, if left to themselves, would care only about safeguarding their own immediate survival. The result would be turmoil – a constant war of everyone against everybody else.

What do you think? What do you consider are the main benefits of having a government, for you as an individual and for the whole of society? Can you think of any dangers or disadvantages?

Think about an average day in your life. Can you identify the ways in which government policy impacts upon your actions? How far do you think the role and influence of government should extend? Are there any areas of life that you think government should not interfere in and if so what are they? Should it be a government's responsibility to provide an education system? Should government determine what is taught and learned in schools? Why?

Policy and culture

Important relationships exist between politics, policy and the collective culture of the population that a government is taken to represent. If a political party is to have much popular support, you might expect it to reflect and support the shared cultural norms, beliefs and values generally held by its public. But as already described, cultures are rarely entirely homogenous. Different values and beliefs may be held within one community and multiple roles or norms accepted and expected within various sectors of society. Within the political community of the nation, an individual's culture may also be impacted upon by things like their ethnicity or religion, their geographical location or socio-economic class. Depending on which sectors of society its members are drawn from, a government may not necessarily reflect an entire population's perspectives, values or beliefs. Indeed, a regular criticism of the policy-making process is that, too often, policies reflect the values and perspectives of only the most powerful social groups (see for example, Taylor *et al.*, 1997).

Reflective Task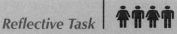

Consider for a moment the composition of your own country's current government. Do you feel they represent an accurate cross-section of your country's population as a whole? Can you find out how many Members of Parliament are women? How many are from ethnic minority backgrounds? What other socio-cultural characteristics do you think most politicians are likely to share? Compile a list of characteristics and discuss these with a partner or small group. Do you think these characteristics might influence the decisions politicians make and if so, in what ways?

(In the British context, a copy of a Commons Library Report (1528) detailing the social background of all members of parliament elected in the 2005 General Election is available for download at **www.parliament.uk**)

We also know that culture is not a static or inherent, already existing thing: cultures are dynamic and are actively produced. The politics and the policies advocated by political parties do not only *reflect* particular cultural perspectives, they can play a very important part in *constructing* culture too.

The decisions that a government makes can have very clear and concrete impacts upon people's lives, as, for example, when formalised into written law. Governments can legislate for or against certain forms of behaviour: no sex, alcohol or cigarettes for under 16s; no violence on television before the watershed; no discrimination in employment on the basis of gender, sexuality, disability, race or age. But government policy can also perform an important symbolic role. Policies present different groups of people and the lives they live in very particular ways. Critically, when a new policy is drafted, it is usually in response to a 'problem' as perceived by those in government: What should we do about the rise in teenage pregnancies? How can we make people feel safer on the streets? How can we increase economic productivity? Or, what should we do to tackle falling standards in schools? Defining a problem entails a value judgement about what constitutes 'normal', or 'desirable' as opposed to 'problematic' situations or behaviours. Policies formalise such judgements and can mobilise resources towards changing things in accord.

Stein (2004, page 3) suggests that policies are best regarded as *systems of thought and action* which *regulate and organise behaviour* through both explicit and implicit means. Policy presents us with a particular way of seeing the world and can provide us with a particular language for talking about it too. In the British context, the term 'ASBO' provides a useful illustration of this. 'ASBOs', 'ASBO culture' and even 'the ASBO Generation' are now a widely understood part of day-to-day and popular vocabularies. 'Anti-Social Behaviour Orders', as they are known in full, are a product of the 1999 Crime and Disorder Act but the acronym is now also used more generally as a shorthand for a certain sort of person – or group of people – whose behaviour is conceived and constructed as unruly, disruptive and/or threatening to the rest of society. Can you think of any popularised 'policy language' circulating in staffrooms or when the general public talk about schools?

Policy, politics and education

Education is essentially a political activity writes Kelly (2004, page 161). In the early 1990s, 4347 members of the British public were asked what they considered the most important roles of government to be. *Almost unanimously*, they answered that, alongside healthcare, the provision of a *good education for everyone* was the most fundamental of a government's responsibilities (Miller *et al.*, 1996, page 39). Indeed, today, access to free, elementary education is formally recognised as a universal human right and it is generally assumed that this is a duty to be undertaken at the level of national government. However, there is no international consensus over how such education should be delivered, or by whom, and it remains entirely open to contest what *an education* – let alone a *good education* – even means (Spring, 2000).

Practical Task

One practical advantage of government taking responsibility for education provision is that, through raising taxes, they have the fiscal resources to provide the necessary infrastructure: to build buildings, to pay teachers, to supply additional materials. What proportion of a national government's total budget might you expect to be spent on providing education? How do you think this might compare to spending in other sectors, for example, spending on defence, spending on the health service or spending on law enforcement?

Make a note of your estimated percentages and then conduct your own research to find accurate statistics for your own government's spending last year. (A summary of British government spending can be found at **www.direct.gov.uk**).

How do you think your government's spending on education compares internationally? Can you find statistics to compare the proportion of public money spent on education in Australia, Sweden, Cuba, the United States, China, Brazil and/or Japan? You may need to compare education spending as a percentage of gross domestic product rather than total government expenditure. A good starting place for statistics is the United Nations Education Science and Culture Organisation website, **www.unesco.org**.

Can you suggest any reasons why the level of spending varies so much internationally?

Historians and political scientists remind us that, in Western Europe, governments first began to take an interest in the provision and control of education systems during the nation-building decades of the nineteenth centuries (see for example Hobsbawm and Gellner, discussed in Chapter 2). In fact, *without state schools, there would be no nations as we know them* today

(Baumann, 2006, page 2). For at the hands of a national government, an education system can perform a number of important political roles. We could characterise such roles as 'policy agendas' for education, different things that a government might want, or intend for, an education system to do. These policy agendas are significant because each can construct 'knowledge', 'learning' and 'learners' in distinct and potentially competing ways.

The economic agenda

The relationship between formal systems of education and the economy has a long historical precedent. Schooling, as well as further and higher education institutions, can be very purposefully oriented towards the transmission of those skills and dispositions that industry and the workforce require. It is no coincidence that the expansion of schooling in Western Europe happened at a time of rapid industrialisation, when new factories were opening requiring a new workforce with at least basic literacy and numeric skills.

In many commentators' analysis, the economic agenda for education intensified in Britain under the Conservative Thatcher government of the 1980s, and continued to occupy a central position in education policy under Prime Minister Tony Blair (1997–2007).

A 1998 Labour Party paper, *The learning Age* makes the centrality of economic considerations clear:

Learning is the key to prosperity for each of us as individuals, as well as for the nation as whole. This is why the Government has put learning at the heart of its ambition.
    Department for Education and Employment (DfEE), 1998, page 1, emphasis added

Today, knowledge itself is regularly framed as a commodity and education an investment as captured in the popular political notion of the 'knowledge economy'.

The social welfare/rights agenda

Formal systems of education can also be used as an arena through which governments can be seen to provide other basic social and welfare needs. Tomlinson (2005) records that in Britain during the mid-twentieth century, the extension of compulsory education was central to the creation of the welfare state. But like many other commentators, she argues that following the economic turbulence and restructuring of the 1970s and 1980s, we now live in a *post welfare society* and this function of education has been marginalised. Nonetheless, recent government emphases on 'joined up thinking' and 'joined up policy delivery' – as for example epitomised by the Every Child Matters legislation, described in further detail below – suggest a reconceptualisation of schools as a focal point for additional government intervention aimed at addressing societies' wellbeing and welfare needs (Raffo and Dyson, 2007).

The social justice agenda

In a similar vein, education can also be presented as a vehicle for promoting social justice: for redistributing resources and opportunities and addressing persistent structural inequalities. A social justice agenda in education would focus on ensuring a system in which everyone could get the most out of their learning experiences, irrespective of differences in parental background, ethnicity, disability or socio-economic class. When the Labour Party came to power in 1997, they made rhetorical commitments to advancing a social justice agenda, both in schools and further afield: issues of 'inclusion' in particular were given significant emphasis. However, critics argue that this was undermined by their greater commitment to market policies of 'choice' and 'competition', which have in fact only exacerbated inequalities (Tomlinson, 2005). At least in the British context, it appears that 'equality' tends to play second fiddle to 'efficiency', 'value for money' and 'accountability' (after David, 2003).

The political agenda

There is also a long historical association between education and what could be characterised as 'political literacy'. For democracy to be effective, it needs an informed (and therefore 'educated'?) electorate. As Stephen Ball usefully highlights, the first major education act in Britain (in 1870) was not unrelated to the 1867 extension of voting rights:

As Robert Lowe (Chancellor of the Exchequer) put it, despite his own ambivalence, the move to a state education system was 'a question of self preservation', the lower classes must be 'educated so that they may appreciate and defer to a higher cultivation when they meet it' and 'to qualify them for the power that has passed . . . into their hands.

Speech in the House of Commons Debate on Education Bill; Ball, 2008, page 63

The Chancellor's comments here neatly illustrate a further potential political function of education: the *domestication* or *cultivation* of the masses and their inculcation into the values and perspectives of the powerful as an exercise in consensus building and control. France (2007, page 85) argues that contemporary British education continues to perform a *regulatory and disciplinary function for those defined outside the parameters of middle-class social acceptability*.

Education can be used to purposefully engender consensus by creating both functional and 'imagined' communities, emphasising cohesion and commonality among what otherwise might be considered (and might consider themselves) a disparate – and potentially divided – collection of individuals and interest groups.

The ideological or moral agenda

The transmission of particular sets of moral and/or ideological values can itself be characterised as a further potential education role. Questions of curriculum content are particularly significant in this respect. As a purposeful selection of what is judged to be 'important' and 'appropriate' knowledge, a curriculum offers perhaps the clearest statement of what a society wants its learners to know and to believe (Apple, 2004). Historically, authoritarian (and anti-democratic) forms of government have exercised the greatest control over what is to be taught in schools. For example, in Soviet Russia during the 1960s, the school curriculum was explicitly used to create a citizenry committed to the ideology of Communism. Rosamund cites a 1964 Soviet report which directed that children should be taught about:

the inevitability of the end of capitalism and the victory of socialism . . . History and society study are important means of bringing the pupils up in a spirit of selfless love for, and devotion to, their socialist motherland.

Cited in Rosamund, 2002, page 72

The report provides illustration of how this imperative was translated into teaching materials for even apparently 'neutral' subjects such as mathematics:

The first cosmonaut was a citizen of the Soviet Union, Comrade Yuri Gagarin. He made a flight around the earth in 108 minutes. How many hours and minutes did the first flight around the earth last?

Rosamund, 2002, page 72

Another remarkable example is taken from an American-funded, primary-level textbook used in Afghanistan between 1986 and 1992:

The speed of a Kalashnikov bullet is 800 metres per second. If a Russian is at a distance of 3200 metres from a mujahid, *and that* mujahid *aims at the Russian's head, calculate how many seconds it will take for the bullet to strike the Russian in the forehead.*

Reproduced in Shirazi, 2007, page 29

This is perhaps a rather extreme illustration, but controversies over curriculum content continue today. In Britain there are regular and recurrent claims that the curriculum has been *corrupted* by *political indoctrination* from the left (Whelan, 2007). It is considered by some to be inappropriately ideological for teaching materials to promote *fashionable causes such as gender awareness, the environment and anti-racism* (Civitas, 2007).

It should be clear that these different agendas for education are not mutually exclusive. Indeed it is likely that more than one will be pursued in government policy at any one time. They regularly overlap and in some cases might reinforce each other; elsewhere they may be held in contradiction with each other or in direct conflict.

The British context

Kelly suggests that the history of education in the United Kingdom reveals a constant swinging *between competing interests and concerns: which might be broadly polarized as a conflict between the claims of society and those of the individual, the vocational and the liberal, the economic and the humanitarian, a national investment and the right of every child, the instrumental and the intrinsic, what education is for and what it is, elitism and egalitarianism, and perhaps, in general, between the possible and desirable, between reality and idealism.*

Kelly, 2004, page 163

In fact, during the nineteenth and early twentieth century, two very different models for education existed side by side. The first reflected the orientation and ethos of the very first schools and universities: private and grammar schools were intended to prepare the sons of the privileged for future leadership. They provided a liberal education to encourage individual's moral, intellectual and academic development. The second model, exemplified by 'elementary' schooling for the masses was intended to produce a workforce with basic skills. The content of this education was initially wilfully restricted to ensure that it *would not give the lower orders ideas above their station* (Lawton, 1975, page 2). The 1944 Butler Education Act was intended to use schooling for egalitarian rather than elitist purposes, providing equality of opportunity for all. However, numerous commentators have reflected that the 'tripartite' model of grammar, technical and secondary modern schools which followed effectively continued to reproduce existing class-based inequalities. Indeed some would argue that *inequality* in opportunity is one of the most enduring characteristics of British education, even today.

Up until the late 1980s, a further key characteristic feature of the British system was the relative autonomy of individual schools and teachers to determine the content of their lessons and the curriculum. As Coulby describes:

There would be guidelines from Local Education Authorities (LEAs) and some loose and infrequent inspection by central government but there were no statutory guidelines as to which subjects should be covered, what material should be dealt with in each subject, what was appropriate to a particular level, how one year's work led into another's, how learning should be planned and assessed, and what feedback on progress should be made to parents and pupils. A teacher with a particular interest in dogs could devise a canine curriculum for a class for an entire term and expect the only response to be the raised eyebrows of colleagues or the head teacher.

Coulby, 2000, page 16

However, the Education Reform Act of 1988 drastically altered the educational landscape by introducing a compulsory national curriculum for all 5–16 year olds in England and Wales. Officially intended to ensure that all pupils would receive a sufficiently broad, balanced and high-quality educational provision, this was an extremely contentious and important policy decision. Like all policy, the Education Reform Act is most instructively examined in relation to the specific social, economic and political context in which it was drawn.

Contemporary culture: policy responses to recent change

The current climate of fluidity and fragmentation, instability and uncertainty emphasised throughout this book has significantly impacted the ways in which politics and policy are deployed. Authoritatively making decisions for society has become increasingly complex: national governments must now respond to challenges of an international nature, whether in terms of the globalised world economy, political security, population movement or the environment. But change is also apparent *within* the boundaries of individual nation-states. A number of interrelated trends which frame domestic policy-making processes are important to highlight here.

The blurring of boundaries between the public and private sectors: networks of governance

In recent years, a number of commentators in Britain and across the world have popularised the term 'governance' to characterise a new set of relationships between the public and governmental systems of power (Rhodes, 1997; Bache, 2003). In particular, they draw attention to the increased role of non-governmental actors and organisations in making and delivering policy. This has also been described as an era of 'new public management' in which some of the power and authority that was once very clearly concentrated at the level of politicians in parliament now appears to be placed in the hands of external consultants and advisory committees, or tendered out to private companies. One indication of this is the rise of 'quasi-autonomous non-governmental organisations', or 'quangos' as they are more commonly known. Within the field of education policy in Britain we could think of organisations such as the Qualifications and Curriculum Authority, the Training and Development Agency, the Learning and Skills Council, or the Student Loans Company among many, many more. Quangos are presented as a more 'flexible' alternative to established government departments which can be *fashioned and refashioned* or *tailored* to a government's specific and changing policy needs (Stott, 2001, page 97, after Weir and Beetham, 1999). Critically, quangos and new public management forms of governance reflect the co-option of principles and practices of private business – chiefly their concerns with 'efficiency' and 'profitability' – into the public sphere. This has taken place as part of a wider set of processes framed as 'modernising' government.

Marketisation and 'choice'

Another way that governments seek to emulate private business models is the introduction of 'quasi-markets' within the public sphere. Here the public is presented as consumers who can choose between competing service providers. 'Diversity' in provision is celebrated and competition for a share of the market is regarded as a stimulus that will improve overall performance and efficiency.

In education policy, the impact of 'choice' and the marketisation of service provision has been especially clear. By 2002, 14 different types of secondary school existed in England alone, each with different funding structures and different statuses, and each offering students different opportunities (France, 2007). The appearance of 'academy schools' as a new choice for parents and students will be examined in further detail below.

In colleges and universities too, further and higher education is presented as a 'commodity' to be bought by students as 'consumers' and delivered by lecturers and teaching staff as 'service providers'. This has considerable consequence for the relationships and expectations between staff and students (as described by Curtis, 2006).

Decentralising and recentralising power: accountability and control

If national governments are devolving some of their responsibilities, does this mean that they are now in a position of less control? Most contemporary critics in Britain do not think so. In fact, many argue that the last three decades have witnessed the *recentralisation* of much national government power. As Clarke (2003, page 214) explains, *managerial responsibility* might well have been devolved to a multitude of institutions and agencies, but central governments still control most financial resources and have developed *an array of evaluative systems* to audit and assess the performance of the service providers they use, against their own set targets and goals.

The role of local as opposed to national government has also been heavily undermined. Again, if we take an example from the field of education policy, during much of the twentieth century, local education authorities (LEAs) had very important roles to play in the direction and delivery of compulsory education in schools. But the Conservative government of the 1980s mounted a series of attacks on local councils and removed many of their educational powers and responsibilities. The 1988 Education Reform Act delivered the most decisive blows: not only did the National Curriculum give increased power to central government but individual schools were also awarded greater autonomy and independence in terms of managing their own financial budgets. Through application for grant maintained status, they were also offered the opportunity to entirely opt out of their LEA. Nor has the position of LEAs under later Labour governments been much improved. Under the premiership of Tony Blair, Labour continued to place its faith in 'target setting' governance. Indeed, LEAs are now themselves subject to the judgement of OFSTED (Office for Standards in Education) inspections. Where they are seen to be underperforming, private sector agencies have been actively recruited to take on their responsibilities (Glatter, 1999).

'Evidence' base

Again influenced by the modernising aspirations of 'efficiency' and 'accountability', increasing attention is now awarded to the 'evidence base' supporting any new or potential policy. One of the mantras of New Labour has been *what matters is what works* and *evidence* is used to illustrate that policy makers are being rational, objective and discerning when they draft new legislation or pilot a new scheme. Most of us would hope that the people who make decisions affecting how others are able to live their lives do so on the basis of information and understanding that is sound: *evidence-based policy making* might well sound like simple common sense. However, remembering the arguments made in Chapter 3, there is cause to feel cautious about claims to 'objectivity' and to knowledge (or 'evidence') that is certain and value free. It is important to reflect on what kinds of 'evidence' are used and presented by policy makers and what sorts of understandings and perspectives are left out. It is also important to consider whether you believe any act of policy making could ever be entirely neutral, and to ask whose interests or concerns the 'evidence' presented actually serves?

Critical Thinking Task

One of the consequences of the modernising agenda of recent government is an over-reliance on statistical 'evidence' that is easy to standardise and compare. An example of this within education policy was the introduction of standardised compulsory testing for all students in England and Wales at ages 7, 11 and 14. The results of the Standard Attainment Tests (or SATs) have subsequently been used as an indicator of school performance and presented in the form of 'league tables' for easily identifying 'successful' or 'failing schools'.

Imagine you are a parent selecting a secondary school for your son or daughter. How influenced would you be by the league tables commonly reproduced in national newspapers? What other kinds of 'evidence' might you require?

Since their introduction following the 1988 ERA, SATs and school league tables have been a regular subject of criticism and controversy. Compile a list of arguments for and against their continued use in schools.

Mediating messages, the role of 'spin'

Evidence bases do not only matter to politicians and other policy makers; the prevalence of a rapidly responsive and easily accessible mass media has added a new dimension to the policy-making process. In recent years, political parties have become increasingly conscious of the ways in which their policies are communicated to and received by the television-watching and newspaper- or blog-reading electorate at home. Gewirtz *et al.* (2004) describe that, in the United Kingdom, Blair's 'New Labour' government was the first to believe that the way in which a policy is presented could influence its ultimate success. Today, all three major political parties are staffed with public relations and press advisors and have 'spin doctors' in their midst. One of the consequences of this is that politicians are concerned to communicate their messages simply and speedily, in snappy, *sound-bite* form (Glatter, 1999; Franklin, 2004). Furthermore, given the pace of contemporary life, *modern politics is all about momentum* as one former speech writer explains (in Ball, 2008, page 2): it is about being seen to be taking action, *transforming* and *innovating* in an attempt to get things done.

With his famous prioritisation of *education, education, education*, Blair ensured that learning became a *major political issue, a major focus of media attention and the recipient of a constant stream of initiatives and interventions from government* (Ball, 2008, page 3). The rate of change within education policy under his government was unprecedented and has only increased in recent years. For those who work at the 'chalkface', such policy 'innovation' can be experienced as a *constant flood of new requirements, changes, exhortations, responsibilities and expectations* (Ball, 2008, page 3). And for those with an interest in analysis of policy frameworks for learning it creates an enormous and amorphous field.

Practical Task

Listen out for discussions of education policy on the radio or television. Can you hear any key terms or phrases being repeated or emphasised? You might want to try keeping a media policy diary, taking note of any new governmental reports or recommendations likely to have an impact on education.

Through library collections and government department websites, it is now very easy to access official policy documents. Some can appear very dense or lengthy but most are accompanied by or begin with an executive statement or summary. Even if you do not read the whole policy document, ask yourself, how easy is it to find out who the authors of this report are? Are there any advisers or consultants listed? And what is the 'evidence' upon which the report is based?

Education policy case studies

The agendas pursued by governments are not always made transparent – they may in fact be wilfully obscured or hidden – but a critical analysis of policy documentation helps to bring them into focus and to uncover the cultures of learning that they help to produce. Amid the significant volume of policy materials released in Britain in recent years, three areas of focus have been chosen for further discussion here: the creation of 'academy' schools, the introduction of a citizenship curriculum and the Every Child Matters agenda. In each case, the long-term impact of these new policies cannot yet be gauged but each reflects particular governmental emphasis and/or concerns that are characteristic of the contemporary period.

Case study 1: the academies programme

Background

Originally announced in 2000, academies can be considered an exemplar of recent policy commitment to and confidence in the market mechanisms of 'diversity' and 'choice'. For a donation of £2 million, a 'sponsor' will go into partnership with the government in establishing and managing a school. Sponsors can name the school and design its buildings; they can also control its board of governors, manage its staff and influence the curriculum that is taught. National government funds its initial construction and running costs. There are currently 83 academies open in England, with a further 150 to be established by the end of 2010.

Implications for contemporary cultures of learning

In keeping with the Labour government's wider educational agenda, academies are established with 'specialist' status and are entitled to select up to 10% of the pupils they admit. As a consequence, both academies and their potential students are framed by the market place: the academies are selling themselves to potential students and their parents in direct competition with other local educational providers, and will do so on the basis of their impressive new buildings, their high-tech resources, their academic specialisms, and their 'unique ethos' as engendered by the sponsors of the school. But arguably it is students who are also commodified, having to sell their aptitudes and their desirability as learners in order to be selected by their first-choice schools.

Government publicity suggests that involving external sponsors in the provision of education will invigorate and innovate where traditional delivery is failing and where cultures of low aspiration have taken hold. Critics, on the other hand, warn that there is no requirement for sponsors to have any educational experience or expertise and that they are free to use academies to pursue religious agendas or business interests. If *no* curriculum is entirely value-free, are we willing to say that anything goes? In a cultural context where multiple, competing perspectives jostle for airspace and attention, where claims to authority are constantly challenged, and where individuals and relationships are increasingly defined in terms of what and how we consume, perhaps it is not surprising that curriculum has itself become a commodity. But should there be limits – other than the £2 million price tag – on who gets to decide what knowledge is 'useful', 'important' or 'true'?

Case study 2: education for citizenship

If the academies programme reflects willingness on the part of policymakers to accept – indeed to encourage – greater variety and fragmentation in terms of education provision, the introduction of a compulsory curriculum for citizenship education can be seen to represent a rather different policy response to diversity.

Background

The 1998 'Crick' report, *Education for Citizenship and the Teaching of Democracy in Schools*, was commissioned as a governmental response to fears of social disengagement and civic apathy among young people in Britain and as an antidote to the perceived corrosive influence of much of contemporary culture as characterised in Chapter 1. In 2002, citizenship education became a statutory requirement of all English secondary schools. It included three distinct strands: *moral and social responsibility*, *community involvement* and *political literacy*. In 2007 it was recommended that a fourth strand be developed, *Identity and diversity: living together in the UK*, intended specifically to address additional and growing concerns that British society was insufficiently 'cohesive' and did not adequately consider itself a united community.

Implications for contemporary cultures of learning

It is left up to individual schools to plan how they will deliver citizenship education: they can do so through dedicated lessons, existing timetabled subject areas, or whole-school activities – as a cross-curricular or extra-curricular theme. Some interpretations of 'active' citizenship, include community engagement and voluntary work, and so 'learning' citizenship does not need to take place in classrooms, nor even necessarily in schools. There is no statutory testing of citizenship at Key Stage 4. As a consequence, citizenship is potentially an especially flexible subject base. Unlike other, longer-established curriculum subjects, it does not face the same pressures to transmit prescribed knowledge for the purposes of passing exams. It could therefore be considered a perfect vehicle for innovation and experimentation in pedagogical practice: the Citizenship Education Review Group (2005) report that the citizenship curriculum can be used to foster and develop critical and engaging, student-centred, learning processes and teaching styles.

However, citizenship education *is* subject to the same scrutiny and surveillance of OFSTED inspections as all other subjects delivered in schools. Early indications from performance reviews suggest that established expectations as to the higher status of discretely timetabled and examined subjects – held by teaching staff as much as by their students – can serve to undermine the position and provision for citizenship education in some schools.

A further-reaching criticism of the current citizenship curriculum concerns its content and the aims and values underpinning the original Crick report. A number of commentators fundamentally challenge the notion that social and moral responsibility and political engagement are things that can or should be taught. Others argue that the citizenship curriculum – as articulated by Crick and his colleagues – is built upon a problematic and unreflexive reverence for established social institutions and values, and in particular the celebration of Britain's version of liberal democracy. They highlight the paradoxes inherent *in teaching citizenship and peaceful 'conflict resolution' during the fighting of a war in Iraq*, and of *teaching 'respect' where government has failed to tackle the causes of poverty* and the *'disrespectful'* behaviours poverty helps produce (Pykett, 2008, page 317). We might also want to consider the tension in claiming and promoting 'equality' and 'justice' as essential British values when British society remains characterised by inequalities and segregations that the education system itself can help produce.

Perhaps a distinction needs to be made between learning *for* politics and political or social engagement, and learning *about* politics. Perhaps learning *for* political and social citizenship in the contemporary context would not be about the transmission or inculcation of already existing and agreed upon values: it could call instead for their constant interrogation and re-evaluation in the light of new pressures and multiple competing points of view; it could encourage and equip young people with the confidence to continue asking questions, rather than attempt to provide them with answers already decided by their teachers or their government.

Case study 3: Every Child Matters and The Children's Plan

Background

Every Child Matters denotes an extensive policy agenda, first outlined in a 2003 DfES Green Paper of the same name and later formalised in the 2004 Children's Act. It was prompted by a report into the death of Victoria Climbié which had tragically highlighted a number of institutional failings in the public service provision intended to support and protect young people and their families. Climbié was murdered by her aunt and her aunt's partner, her legal guardians while living in Britain, but in the months before her death she had been brought to the attention of the police, social services and the National Health Services, each of whom had noted signs of ongoing abuse but none of whom were able to adequately intervene.

Every Child Matters (ECM) emphasises the importance of multi-sector collaboration. To reflect this, in 2007, the new government Department for Children, Families and Schools was created, and a further policy report was produced. The five key outcomes of ECM (being healthy; staying safe; enjoying and achieving; making a positive contribution; achieving economic wellbeing) were supplemented by *The Children's Plan*, which further outlines how the government intends to achieve its vision of improving children's lives.

Implications for contemporary cultures of learning

Both Every Child Matters and The Children's Plan have especially significant impacts for schools. Within the classroom, conceptions of learning are broadened: both documents ask for an emphasis on personalised learning and assessment rather than systems that are standardised. They also stress the importance of young people acquiring *social and emotional skills*. Outside of classrooms – and after standard teaching hours – the function of schools themselves is 'extended': here schools are positioned as a focal point for additional child and community services: study support, activity groups, access to specialist health and/or welfare advice.

Response to the Every Child Matters agenda has been largely enthusiastic; its ethos of collaboration, personalisation and inclusion, perhaps unsurprisingly, echoes the value positions and concerns of many individuals who work in schools (Tutt, 2006).

However, other commentators are once again concerned that schools' (and ultimately the government's) ability to achieve these goals are undermined by the *tables, targets and tests regime* which continues to dominate the framing and funding of schools (Tutt, 2006). Rona Tutt asks us to remember the five objectives of *Every Child Matters* and to consider each in relation to the impact of SATs- and 'standards'-oriented learning that the logic of the league tables demands:

1 *Is it healthy to hothouse all pupils into passing tests and exams for which they may not be ready or cut out?*
2 *Does it help to make children feel safe in schools, when they are under pressure to reach certain levels they know they cannot reach however hard they try?*
3 *Does it help them to enjoy school when the so-called 'Achievement and Attainment Tables' (commonly known as 'league tables') recognise the attainment of some rather than the achievements of all, and when the broader curriculum that gives them a better chance of achieving gets crowded out by an emphasis on getting children through tests?*
4 *Does it enable them to feel they are making a positive contribution to their school when, in terms of a narrow range of results, they are branded sub-standard?*
5 *Does it help them to become economically independent when academic worth is rated above all other abilities, including the ability to form relationships, to show qualities of leadership, to work as part of a team, to master practical, sporting or artistic skills, all of which may help them in the workplace?* (Tutt, 2006, page 214).

Nor have all of the policies proposed within the Every Child Matters agenda been equally well received: coercive – or even disciplinary – measures to ensure parents take responsibility for their children have proven especially contentious. Some critics consider that the extension of schooling can in fact be regarded as an inappropriate and unjustified extension of government regulation, surveillance and control (Williams, 2004; Pykett, 2008).

Chapter Summary

After reading this chapter, you should recognise that:

- Education can be used by government for a number of instrumental economic, social and/or political roles, and competing governmental agendas offer alternate constructions of 'education', 'knowledge' and of what it means to learn.
- Relationships of power between 'the public', 'the government' and 'the market economy' are becomingly increasingly complex. This has considerable impact on the sorts of education policies that currently dominate.
- Recent directions taken by educational policy makers in Britain offer contradictory opportunities and obstacles. However, many commentators consider that over-reliance upon the logic of the market economy in education – creating a regime of 'tests, tables and targets' – undermines and can threaten the viability of alternative understandings of learning and of schools.

Research focus

Background

Two, very useful introductory texts are:

- Ball, S (2008) *The education debate: policy and politics in the twenty-first century*. Bristol: Policy Press.
- Tomlinson, S (2005) *Education in a post-welfare society*. Maidenhead: Open University Press.

Both Ball and Tomlinson are clearly critical of the roles that market economics have played in education policy in recent years. Can you summarise their main concerns? You might also want to consider exploring alternative points of views. Michael Barber is a prominent advocate of recent educational reform as outlined in:

- Barber, M (1997) *The learning game: arguments for an education revolution*. London: Indigo.

Education policy case studies

Each of the three case studies introduced in this chapter could be explored in much greater detail. Original policy documents including Green and White Papers as well as Advisory Committee reports and research briefings are easily available from the Department for Children, Schools and Families website, **www.dcsf.gov.uk**.

All three areas of policy focus have attracted considerable attention and commentary from academics, from practitioners and from the national media. Focusing on one of the three case studies suggested, investigate the response from each of these groups. You could use the books and articles referenced in this chapter as a starting point for academic perspectives and use contributions to journals such as the *Times Educational Supplement* (TES), or *Forum: for promoting 3–19 comprehensive education* to examine practitioner views. From each group's perspective, what are the most significant benefits and/or limitations or dangers presented by the policy? Do you think the policy is likely to be successful in achieving its intended aims?

Curriculum

The chapter suggested that questions of curriculum were especially interesting in exploring the ideological function that can be performed by schools. In fact, curriculum studies could be considered a distinct and important subfield within education policy. A seminal work is:

- Apple, M (2004) *Ideology and curriculum*, 3rd edition. London: Routledge.

We have seen that in Britain there is one centralised, national curriculum. What do you think are the advantages of this and what are its potential challenges and limitations? Kelly (2004) provides a useful critical discussion (see especially Chapter 8):

- Kelly, AV (2004) *The curriculum: theory and practice*, 5th edition. London: Sage.

Chapter 6

In classrooms and corridors:
a sociological approach

Learning outcomes

By the end of this chapter you should be able to:

- recognise how processes such as 'role allocation', 'labelling' and teacher or peer-group expectation contribute to a 'hidden curriculum' in schools;
- understand what is meant by a 'stratified society' and suggest possible links between formal education and persistent social inequalities;
- illustrate that the experience of schooling can vary for students from different social groups;
- assess the argument that young people today are freer than ever before to be and become whomever they want to be.

Chapter outline

In this chapter you will examine the learning encounters that take place between staff and students in schools by drawing on theoretical argument and empirical research from the academic discipline of sociology. In the simplest terms, sociology is the study of how human societies work. Sociologists try to find and explain patterns in the way that people relate to and interact with each other and look for underlying 'systems' or 'structures' that can influence individuals' actions, attitudes and opportunities.

Education has a long history as a key sociological concern. In particular, sociologists have argued that education can serve to allocate specific roles and status positions to members of different social groups. In so doing, schools have been blamed for reproducing 'stratifications' in society, that is, they are seen to help perpetuate a number of forms of inequality between individuals marked by group identities such as race or ethnicity, gender and socio-economic class. It is important to examine and expand upon these claims.

However, it has also been argued that dramatic recent changes in our economic, political and cultural lives have been so significant and so extensive that the social structures and grouped identities that sociologists traditionally describe are no longer as stable – nor, perhaps, as important – as they once were. The chapter concludes by considering these arguments, asking to what extent are 'old' sociological theories of education still relevant? What does a twenty-first-century educational sociology look like? And what is its value to those concerned with learning and teaching today?

What did you learn at school today? Looking at classrooms through the lens of sociology

Sociology is concerned with everyday experience: we all live and do the things that sociologists think and write about. A school, for example, is, for the majority, a very familiar concept: most people have a commonsense understanding of what a school is and what schools do. However, a sociological perspective aims to go beyond 'commonsense' or everyday under-standings, and questions what may at first seem 'only natural' or 'obvious' (Bauman and May, 2001). A commonsense perspective might assume that people go to school because there they will learn skills and acquire knowledge that will help them 'get on' in later life (Andersen and Taylor, 2005). A commonsense perspective might also assume that *what* people learn in schools is clearly laid out in timetables and lesson plans – a curriculum of subject areas: 'English', 'maths', 'French', perhaps even 'sociology'.

Certainly there is some truth in both of these commonsense assumptions. However, from a sociological perspective, writers have argued that for some groups of students, the experience of schooling can serve only to hold them back. Others have shown that it is not only knowledge about English, maths or other formal curriculum areas that students acquire in school. Indeed, from a sociological perspective, a school is a fascinating arena in which many complex social interactions, negotiations and interpretations take place and where a multitude of hidden, often unintended 'lessons' are learned.

As its title indicates, the primary focus of this chapter is the 'micro' level of education: face-to-face encounters 'in classrooms and corridors'. However, the chapter argues that the most useful sociological analyses are able to make connections between the 'micro-level' experi-ences of individuals and wider, or more generalised, 'macro-level' relationships and processes. The chapter therefore begins with a discussion of 'macro-level' sociological theories con-cerning the interrelationships between society and schools. Often sociology textbooks make a clear separation between 'old' macro-level theory work and newer micro-level classroom research, but this chapter draws regular connection between the two.

The 'functionalist' perspective on schools

The French scholar Emile Durkheim was a very important figure in twentieth century sociology; he was also one of the first sociologists to pay significant attention to education and schools. Durkheim's sociology has been characterised as a 'functionalist' or 'consensus' approach. He believed that society was best understood as an organised system made up of interlocking and interdependent parts. You could draw a parallel here with a living organism such as the human body. Each organ in the body performs its own individual functions upon which all the other organs – and the body as a whole – depend. For Durkheim and other functionalist sociologists, the 'organs' of society were its social institutions, for example the family, religion, work-life, government, the legal system and – most importantly for our current discussion – education and schools. To understand the significance of any one of these institutions, Durkheim believed you had to understand the part it plays – or the 'function' it performs – in relation to society as a whole (Durkheim, 2003; see also Walford 2004).

What functions then, does a school perform for society? One very practical function is to equip students with the skills needed to become workers in the wider economy. Indeed, Talcott Parsons, another key functionalist sociologist, suggested that formal education should *be regarded as a series of apprenticeships for adult occupational roles* (Parsons, 1964, page 240). But Durkheim believed that schools also performed a vital moral, disciplinary and socialising role.

Education as 'systematic socialisation'

Although Durkheim recognised that societies can and do change over time, he saw the primary function of education as perpetuating existing social systems rather than transforming them in any radical way (another key hallmark of functionalist sociology is its depiction of society as something characterised by order and relative stability). As has been described, societies reproduce themselves by transmitting shared knowledge, cultural values and expectations in a variety of informal and often unexamined ways: 'socialisation' – those processes through which we learn how to be a human within our own specific culture and society – actually begins long before formal schooling, within the family and at home. However, Durkheim considered it important to distinguish between this informal learning or early socialisation, and 'education' as the officially sanctioned, institutionalised learning – or 'systematic socialisation' – that takes place within schools.

For Durkheim, a school, unlike a family, was a community where people would be brought together not because they were related, or because they liked each other, but for abstract and instrumental reasons. Schools were *colder and more impersonal* than family life and represented an important intermediary space between what Durkheim described as the *affective morality* of the family (based on feelings and personal preferences) and the *rigorous morality of civic life* (which had to be impartial and detached) (Durkheim, 2003, page 149). In a collection of essays published after his death, Durkheim emphasises the importance for society of schools' adherence to firm discipline and clear rules. These, he argued, were not simply a matter of creating order to make life easier for teaching, nor simply an expression of teachers' power over the students in their class. Rather he felt that:

It is by respecting the school rules that the child learns to respect rules in general, that he develops the habit of self-control and restraint simply because he should control and restrain himself. It is a first initiation into the austerity of duty. Serious life.

Durkheim, 2003, page 149

Durkheim believed that these were essential qualities to develop and that it was through the discipline of the classroom that students would learn to situate themselves within society. Like Hobbe's description of human life without government as *nasty, brutish and short*, Durkheim compares a class without discipline to an unruly and destructive mob. He considers that it is in each individual's best interest to see themselves as *social beings* – just one part of a wider group – and to take responsibility for this, adapting their own behaviour in accord. Social behaviour demands that individuals are willing to curb their own individualism and 'conform' to the rules and expectations that govern their society. Recalling arguments presented earlier in this book, Durkheim suggested that in *simpler*, pre-industrial societies, group members automatically shared a strong *conscience collective* – that is, a sense of common interest and shared beliefs. However, in modern, complex societies, such a conscience has to be actively produced. It is this *conscience collective* – or *consensus* – production that Durkheim identifies as a key function of formal education and schools.

Education as allocation for specific roles

In addition to instilling a sense of solidarity, functionalist sociologists regard that schools aid the smooth function of society by helping students identify and prepare for 'appropriate' social and vocational roles. Not only should schools provide students with a set of general skills needed for all employment, part of schools' function for society is to direct the 'right sorts' of student towards the 'right sorts' of jobs. Talcott Parsons was especially clear in this respect:

schools were responsible for the allocation of social roles. This is a very important idea because it suggests that schools, in addition to transmitting a cultural *sameness* – those shared values and common interests already emphasised – should also actively cultivate students' *difference*, in terms of their aspirations as well as their competencies and skills.

Critically for Parsons, school should provide the mechanisms through which an individual's usefulness for society is formally assessed. He argued it was in the whole of society's best interests if the 'best' – most talented? most hardworking? – individuals could be identified and given the opportunity to perform society's 'most important' roles. From this perspective, formal education is intimately bound up with the allocation of 'status' as well as the allocation of roles. Parsons suggested that in informal settings such as the family or social group, an individual's social status was likely to be *ascribed* on the basis of involuntary factors such as being someone's daughter and someone else's older sister, being a teenager, or being 'white British' or African-Caribbean. In schools however, objective criteria should be employed to ensure that 'status' – as ultimately reflected in exam success – was *achieved* on the basis of an individual's talent, effort and aptitude. Writing of America during the 1950s, Parsons believed that schools reflected meritocratic principles shared by wider society. If education offered a truly level playing-field – as he thought was true – and an individual failed to achieve their ambitions or full potential, they had only themselves to blame. If everyone had equal opportunities, both those who were successful and those who failed by comparison would accept as fair the resulting social position they were able to occupy. If different positions within society are marked by different status – different access to wealth, power and prestige – sociologists describe that society as 'stratified'.

Critical Thinking Task

Perhaps it will not surprise you to hear that Talcott Parson's functionalist sociology of education has received considerable criticism. Some of the terms he uses sound very problematic. Why do you think that might be? Who do you think gets to decide what an 'appropriate' role for an individual student is, what the 'right' student or 'best' student means, or what are considered the 'most important' positions for people to occupy?

Do you think that today's schools, and today's society is 'meritocratic', with success and status dependent upon individual talent and hard work? Do you think there is a relationship between 'achieved' and 'ascribed' status? What evidence could you call upon to support the answer you give?

Social roles, social groups and social identity

Before we examine some alternative sociological perspectives on education, it is useful to consider in a little more detail the notion of a social role or social status and the related concepts, 'social identity' and 'social group'. This task is not aided by the frustrating reality that sociologists and other social scientists use each of these terms in inconsistent, sometimes interchangeable ways.

Most commonly, the idea of a social role is used to suggest that the way in which a person behaves has more to do with the position and status they occupy within a social system – sometimes understood as the 'social group' that they belong to – than with their individual dispositions or personality. Each society – and each social institution – will offer a different repertoire of varied roles for individuals to perform. You could think of 'university lecturer' as one such role. Independently of all the many individuals who have taught in universities, it is very likely that even before your very first lecture, you had certain expectations as to how a university lecturer would, or *should*, behave. On your first morning of classes, you perhaps quickly and unthinkingly identified that your lecturer was likely to be the person standing at the front of the room. You may also have made the reasonable assumption that this lecturer would be able to talk to you knowledgeably about a subject for a set period of time and you could legitimately feel disappointed if this was not the case. Although it could have been frustrating at first, you were perhaps not altogether surprised if the lecturer used especially complicated or technical-sounding vocabulary (you may have reacted differently, however, if this was how a friend started talking to you on a Friday night visit to the pub). Sitting, pen in hand or lap-top open in a lecture theatre, you had probably also internalised and accepted expectations of how you, as 'student' should behave.

A lecture is likely to run most smoothly if both lecturer and student are aware of, willing and able to demonstrate the behaviours and attitudes expected of – and considered appropriate for – their own respective roles. For functional sociologists, this is how to envision the whole of society. Thinking in terms of 'roles' and 'performances' emphasises the extent to which apparently individual and personal behaviours are heavily influenced by social context and by deeply internalised understandings of what, and who, other people expect us to be.

In the university-based example, both lecturer and student have exercised a degree of choice in deciding to occupy their specific positions. However, the extent to which individuals are free to determine exactly which roles they perform is a further important sociological – and educational – concern. For not all social roles are freely chosen. Roles can be assigned to us by other people and they can also be inherited at birth.

Assigned roles – labelling in schools

In the context of a classroom, the two most immediately obvious roles are those of 'teacher' and 'pupil' or 'student'. 'Teachers' could be considered to occupy a position of power in relation to their pupils in a number of different ways (Cohen, 2002). In most societies, an 'adult' is already in a privileged position over a 'teenager' or 'child'. It is teachers who decide how most of a student's time is spent while in their classrooms, teachers who are the voice of authority over classroom discipline and teachers who are the arbiters of what knowledge is legitimate and appropriate for students to learn. Classroom-based sociological research also indicates that teachers can exercise considerable further power by allocating additional roles to their students through official and unofficial 'labels' in both deliberate and unintended ways.

Influential research by Keddie (1971) and Becker (1952) suggests that teachers enter classrooms with an 'ideal type' of student in their mind. This student is likely to be hard-working, courteous and conscientious as well as academically able. The 'ideal type' can then act as an informal benchmark against which real-life students are judged. Behaviours that do not fit the model are labelled 'deviant'. The labels used to describe specific acts of behaviour can quickly become attached to individual students but there is a very important distinction between thinking of, and talking about 'bad behaviour' on one hand and 'bad kids' on the other. As Chapman (1986, page 112) describes:

Labelling has a social-control effect. Being labelled for a minor transgression of the rules may effectively stop the pupil from repeating that transgression. But labelling can also amplify deviant behaviour. Hargreaves (1976) describes how labelling assigns a new status to a pupil. He/she is no longer treated as 'normal' but as a potential 'problem'. The deviant act committed by the pupil comes to engulf them. The pupil starts to develop a self-concept based on the label, which in turn reinforces the label.

The important point is that the judgements and expectations made by teachers get communicated to students in various ways. Consider the following reflections from staff and students at one secondary school:

Yeah, no, it's like, the people who've got their label like . . . like me and Dan will have the label of being, confident and, like, mouthy. So, from that, every teacher will know about it. Like, they discuss it in the staffroom, and then, so every teacher knows about it, which means, their opinion on you, would be like, 'you're being loud' and not . . . never different. But it depends on how the teacher treats you, how you act.

They just like talk about what's happened – in the staffroom. And then when they're like . . . you have an argument with a teacher, they'll say 'well I'm not the only one that thinks it', em, 'it's everyone in the staffroom'. That sort of comment, that just doesn't need to be there.

Layla, Year 10

It sounds a bit terrible, but you can end up feeling like you are using the 'good kids' as pawns, you know, between the trouble makers, organising the class so it goes 'good kid, bad kid, good kid, bad.

Miss Platt, history teacher

Such labels matter. Forty years' worth of sociological research suggests that teacher expectations can have a 'self-fulfilling prophecy' effect. A famous study by Rosenthal and Jacobsen in 1968 illustrated that if a teacher believed a student *could* perform effectively, they were likely to treat them in such a manner that actually encouraged their ultimate success. At the same time, a student who is regularly labelled 'badly behaving' or 'low ability' may eventually accept the authority of their teacher's judgement and give up trying to act in any other way. Ball (1981) argues that streaming students by (perceived) ability has a similar effect.

Practical Task

Think about the mechanics of how a 'self-fulfilling prophecy' works. Can you construct two different imaginary cycles that begin with a teacher labelling an individual student as (a) 'bright', 'good', 'with potential' and (b) 'unintelligent', 'bad', 'unlikely to succeed'. Using the framework in Figure 6.1, in each case consider how both the teacher and student's feelings and actions might be influenced. Can you identify ways in which the self-fulfilling prophecy could be prevented from coming true?

Ascribed roles: gender, race, ethnicity and social class in school

Another important observation made by sociologists of education is that teachers' judgements, and the interpretations they make of behaviour and ability, are regularly influenced by other aspects of students' social identities. Not all roles are achieved, that is given to us on the basis

Figure 6.1 Cycle of behaviour resulting from labelling

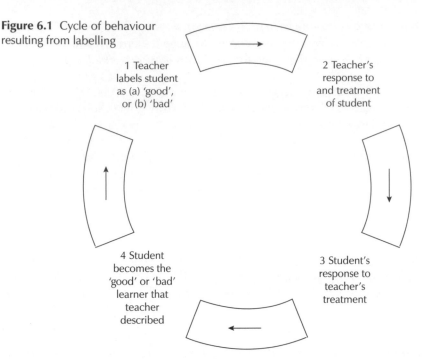

1 Teacher labels student as (a) 'good', or (b) 'bad'

2 Teacher's response to and treatment of student

3 Student's response to teacher's treatment

4 Student becomes the 'good' or 'bad' learner that teacher described

of things we do (the choices we make, the effort we put in or the behaviours that we display). Some are ascribed to us on the basis of contingencies of our birth such as our gender, our race or ethnicity, our socio-economic class background, our sexual orientation, and whether or not we have a mental or physical disability. There are powerful expectations and encouragements for individuals from different groups within society to behave in different ways.

For example, biological 'sex' refers to the physical body that an individual is born with, for most people either 'male' or 'female'. 'Gender' on the other hand refers to socially constructed expectations for male and female behaviour characterised as 'masculinity' and 'femininity'. While biology may determine that there are anatomical and genetic differences between boys and girls or men and women, sociologists argue that it is *not* on the basis of biology that more boys than girls play football, that men are seen to make better plumbers or that only girls and women are expected to wear make up and skirts. Instead, each of these things are considered a consequence of powerful 'gender roles'.

Both sociological and psychological research shows that children internalise an understanding of 'appropriate' gender roles from a very young age (Bem, 1989; Gove and Watt, 2000). They are likely therefore to arrive at school with already embedded ideas about how 'boys' and 'girls' should behave. Schools however, can reinforce – or may be able to challenge – children's gendered identity. Sociological research in Britain throughout the 1980s and 1990s recorded that both the official and hidden curriculum encouraged girls to adopt and identify themselves with subservient and submissive roles. Kelly (1986) provides a useful summary of classroom studies on teacher–student interaction concluding that, very consistently, girls received less teacher attention than boys: girls received less criticism from their teachers, but received less personalised instruction too. MacIntosh (1990) also suggests that girls themselves are often aware of this discrepancy and are encouraged to consider their position in the classroom – and potentially in wider society – as less important than boys. Lessons about gender are also learned where school structures reflect a gendered division of labour: if all the staff in the school canteen are dinner *ladies*, if there are very few women teaching science-based or technical subjects, or if the senior and management staff are predominantly male.

Nor is it only teachers' preconceptions that help reproduce distinct gender roles. Peer-group expectations are very influential too. This is particularly apparent where students are asked to choose the subjects they will study in the last years of school. Here girls report being reluctant to opt for academic subjects that will make them appear 'unfeminine' (Francis, 2000). Although recent research and commentary has focused on boys' overall underachievement in school examinations, the subject areas in which male students continue to be concentrated, especially at advanced levels, are those likely to translate into the jobs that continue to be most valued and better financially rewarded by society.

The labels used and expectations created or reinforced through schooling matter, because they can help to determine where individuals find themselves positioned within wider society. If society expects and encourages women to be less ambitious, less self-assured, more domestic and more caring towards others than men, and if this is reflected in the way that teachers approach and respond to female students in their classrooms, fewer girls than boys are likely to find themselves in high-status, professional roles.

Conflict theories of education and the reproduction of social class

Introductory sociology textbooks regularly compare functionalist perspectives on education with theories described as 'conflict' accounts. As the name suggests, where functionalists characterise social systems in terms of order, consensus and harmonious stability, conflict theorists see society and its educational provision as sites of conflict, division and inequality. In particular, drawing heavily upon the arguments of the German socialist Karl Marx, they consider the most fundamental divisions in society to be those that are built upon social class.

Reflective Task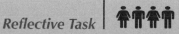

How confidently are you able to define 'social class'? How many social classes do you think there are in your society? And which do you think you belong to? Although commentators, including academics, regularly refer to 'middle' and 'working class' groups of people, these terms have never been officially defined. In Britain, people interested in recording and comparing statistics, tend to use something called the Registrar General's Scale which actually lists six distinct classes (one of which is further subdivided) based on the skill level required for different occupational roles:

I   Professional
II   Managerial/technical
III(a) Skilled (non-manual)
III(b) Skilled (manual)
IV   Partly skilled
V   Unskilled
VI   Other

In your group can you identify where on the Registrar General Scale the following occupations could be found?

* university professor;
* refuse collector;
* receptionist;

- electrician;
- professional footballer;
- piano player;
- learning support assistant;
- politician;
- bank manager;
- nurse;
- dancer.

Now try to estimate both the annual salary and minimum educational qualification needed for each of these occupations? Do you notice any patterns? Can you identify any problems or limitations with this scale?

Apart from salary and occupation, the following factors have also been associated with social class. Which do you think could be used as the most reliable markers of class identity? Can you add any more of your own?

- the supermarket and shops that people commonly visit;
- the newspaper they choose to read;
- the accent they speak in and the vocabulary they use;
- the clothes they wear;
- the political party they vote for;
- the number of cars they own;
- the value of their house and whether it is owned by them, by the council or by a private landlord.

It is significant to remember that in its very first incarnations, and for a long time after, formal education was a provision offered only to the sons of society's elite. Even when education was eventually extended to the general masses, its architects envisioned a differentiated system whereby the working population would receive the basic skills needed for vocational apprenticeship, while a more academic, liberal education would remain the preserve of the rich and the privileged. Conflict theory suggests that such educational inequality continues to exist.

In one of the best-known examples of a conflict theory perspective, Bowles and Gintis (1976) draw a parallel between the role of education in reproducing inequalities between rulers and slaves in the Ancient world, lords and peasants in Medieval Europe and the professional and working classes of capitalist society in twentieth-century America. Far from believing in Talcott Parson's meritocracy, they argue that the conformity and discipline instilled by formal schooling actually only serve to produce a docile and compliant source of cheap labour: the aspirations and potential of individuals are subservient to the needs and demands of the economy. In schools, students from less privileged backgrounds learn to accept existing social hierarchies. Acquiescence to authority, however unfair it may initially seem, is presented as the only route to educational and vocational success.

This is clearly a very critical interpretation of formal education; you could also argue that it is an unduly pessimistic and determinist account. Within existing educational systems, Bowles and Gintis imply that there is very little hope for working class children and, outside of a Marxist revolution, little hope for possible change. Furthermore, if schools *only* serve to reproduce and reinforce the dominance of those who are already powerful, what does this say about the work that teachers do? Stephens *et al.* (1998, page 206) make the important point that conflict theories:

seem to suggest that school teachers 'conspire' with the ruling class to ensure that some children are primed for leadership and others for servitude. Speaking as teachers, we don't regard our role as one of colluding with the rich and powerful in an attempt to provide different learning cultures for future leaders and servants.

Do you consider it likely that many teachers do? Conflict theories also have a tendency to present working class children as helpless victims, powerless against the dominant social system in which they find themselves. This in itself is not a very helpful or flattering view.

The sociological concepts of 'structure' and 'agency' are useful to examine here. When sociologists talk of social systems, grouped identities and institutions, they are talking about real and perceived (social) *structures* that exert an influence upon individuals' lives. But the individuals themselves are still an important part of this picture, albeit one that can get lost in some early sociological accounts. No one person's behaviour is *entirely* determined by social structures as conflict theory appears to suggest. We can all act unpredictably, we all have our own different interpretation of social situations and we all have at least a degree of independence and choice. '*Agency*' refers to the capacity of individuals to act freely and make their own independent decisions. To more fully explore the interplay of structure and agency – and to understand why, in spite of individual teachers' stated commitment to social justice, class-based and other inequalities in education continue, regularly, to exist – it is instructive to return our attention to closer examination of the micro-scale interactions and encounters experienced in school. This is precisely the project attempted by two twentieth-century sociologists, Basil Bernstein and Pierre Bourdieu.

The importance of language: 'restricted' and 'elaborated' codes

The British sociologist Basil Bernstein focused much of his attention on how the forms of language commonly used among certain groups of students could facilitate – or prohibit – school-based learning taking place (Bernstein, 1996). In essence, he argued that formal education is conducted primarily in the language of the middle classes, placing middle-class children at a distinct advantage in their communication with teachers and marginalising other groups. Drawing upon empirical research conducted in classrooms, Bernstein suggested that the working class children he encountered were more likely to have grown up in close-knit, localised communities. As a consequence, he reported that most used a style of language that assumed a high degree of familiarity with implicit meanings that were not always easily intelligible to those outside of the immediate surrounds. He described these forms of language in terms of their 'restricted code'. Bernstein argued that middle class home lives on the other hand, were likely to be characterised by greater mobility in social, cultural and geographic terms. Middle-class children were therefore more familiar with using language to articulate abstracted and universal principles or ideas through an 'elaborated code'. When schools emphasise the value of dealing with abstract and objective, rather than context dependent or local, particularist knowledge – or privilege 'elaborated' over 'restricted' codes for communication – they make it harder for working class children to succeed.

Sociological accounts of student experience in classrooms continue to indicate the salience of some of Bernstein's claims. For example, Cooper (1998) details how a group of primary school-aged children approach mathematics test questions framed around 'real-world' examples in very different ways. One such question presented students with two pie-chart illustrations depicting the proportion of different types of socks worn to school one day by girls and boys.

Ann says, 'More girls than boys wore patterned socks' the question states. 'Using both graphs give as many reasons as you can why she is right.

Cooper 1998, page 516

'Diane' whom Cooper describes as 'middle class' and of 'high ability' interprets and approaches the question exactly as the examiners intended: she compares the abstracted statistics that each chart represents. 'Mike' on the other hand, who *is working class and of average measured 'ability', falls straight into the trap laid by the question's familiar,* 'real-world' context. He draws inappropriately – as regards the question – on his own, context specific observations and experience.

Mike: Is it – I think, really, boys just wear, like, plain old sporty socks –

Unless they're like, teachers' pet [. . .] But the girls, the girls seem to have more pattern on their socks [. . .] The boys have just got old sporty things with something like sport written down them.

As Cooper's discussion continues, we hear that, when invited to, Diane is also able to draw upon her own experience. However, she appears to intuitively know that this is *not* the form of knowledge 'appropriate' in the context of a maths lesson. Cooper's analysis suggests that this is a consequence of her 'middle-classness' and her familiarity with the use of elaborated codes.

Cultural capital

Pierre Bourdieu's work extends some of the arguments of Bernstein to demonstrate that the economic and political inequalities that concern conflict theorists of education are culturally as well as materially reproduced (Bourdieu and Passeron, 1977). He employs the concept of 'cultural capital' to demonstrate that an individual's cultural background should be considered in terms of the resources it provides. However, he also emphasises that not all backgrounds – or reserves of cultural capital – are valued equally by society, or by teachers in schools. It is not only the language codes of working class children that are misunderstood or undermined in classroom contexts but their whole way of understanding and making sense of the world: their attitudes and expectations, dispositions and tastes.

Bourdieu argues that the 'ideal type' of student imagined by teachers is modelled on middle-class values, expectations and experiences: it is therefore a role that is much easier for middle-class children to perform. In fact, he argues that whole schools are saturated with middle- and upper-class culture, so much so that working class children – as well as those from minority ethnic backgrounds – are likely to feel immediately out of place, not yet aware of, or able to master, the rules of the game that other students seem so easily to know how to play.

It is very important to emphasise that, in spite of the criticisms levelled at Bernstein in particular, neither he nor Bourdieu intended to locate the blame for certain students' comparative academic failure with their families or cultural backgrounds (i.e. in 'inadequately' preparing their children for school). Instead, both writers wanted to recognise the importance of cultural difference and argued that it was the education system itself, and the interpretations or misunderstandings of teachers, that turned 'difference' into 'disadvantage' or 'deficit'.

'Counter-cultural' capital: the possibility of resistance

It is also important to remember that teachers are not the only source of authority and judgement operating within a school. Peer-group censure or approval and the interactions between students are sociologically important too: the cultural capital valued and rewarded by teachers and in examinations is not the only form that circulates. Studies by Corrigan (1979) and Willis (1977) describe clear 'counter-cultural' communities operating within classroom contexts where acceptance and approval by members is dependent on behaviours and attitudes that are directly oppositional to those demanded by the school.

As Cohen interprets:

[For] kids that simply do not see the world in the same way as the school [the] *'problem' is how to resist and protect themselves from an alien imposition, not how to attain its values.*

Cohen, 1997, page 152

And so for example, 'the lads' that Willis spent 18 months with at a comprehensive school in 'Hammertown', openly recognise that they are never going to be 'successful' by their teachers' standards and so turn to each other for an alternative source of validation and esteem. Students who conform to teachers' expectations are derisively labelled 'ear oles': 'the lads' by contrast are committed to subverting and rejecting all that the school represents. Their time in class is spent earning respect from each other by finding new ways to skilfully disrupt lessons, to do as little work as is possible and to 'have a laff'. However, as Willis also noted, the last laugh was perhaps still with the boys' teachers, as it is through academic qualifications – still an important route to career success and future prospects – that cultural capital could be exchanged for economic and political power.

Classroom-based research with disparate groups of students reminds us that the behavioural and academic expectations of teachers are not the only demands that young people have to negotiate. Even for students who are not as wilfully 'anti-schooling' as Willis' 'lads', schools are a complex social environment in which different aspects of identity are developed and performed. In their study of schooling, 'race' and masculinity among 11–14 year olds in London, Frosh *et al.* (2002) make this very clear. As Phoenix (2004, page 232) emphasises, educators often underestimate the ways in which individuals regulate their identities as learners in relation to social interactions and pressures that do not involve their teacher, indeed, of which their teachers may not even be aware.

Practical Task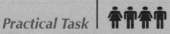

Richardson and Wood (2000) provide a useful summary of possible tensions between 'street culture' – which they argue heavily influences many young people – and the cultural norms and expectations officially sanctioned within school.

Look at Table 6.1. In partners or small groups can you fill in the gaps in this table? For, example, what do you think the official school perspective on responding to provocation is? Although Richardson and Wood describe competing perspectives on masculinity, they remain quiet on how girls are expected to behave. Again, can you offer suggestions of the dominant view, both within the school and on the street?

Table 6.1 'Street culture' versus school culture (adapted from Richardson and Wood 2000, page 20)

	'Street culture' – expectations and norms	School culture – expectations and norms
Demeanour, posture, gestures, etc.	Body language used to show you expect to be respected or that you challenge the authority of others (e.g. slouching, 'kissing teeth', walking with a swagger).	Body language and general attitude should show you accept 'the role of pupil'. Respect and defer to authority, tradition, the rules (e.g. sitting up straight in class and keeping all four legs of the chair on the ground).
Provocation	Retaliate first . . . shoot from the hip . . . swear and use verbal abuse . . . signal you're ready to use force . . . use force (fists, weapons) if necessary.	?
Clothing, possessions	Fashionable, expensive clothes and objects show: (a) that you are able to afford them; (b) that you are confident no-one will dare to try and take them away from you. Express your personality and earn you respect.	?
View of conflict	Always try to win or risk losing face.	?
Masculinity	You show you're a man by being hard, bad, cool: • not being a swot or boffin; • not showing vulnerability, anxiety, tenderness, affection; • showing contempt for homosexuality; • being respected, never losing face, defying authority; • taking risks, maybe dicing with death.	?
Femininity	?	?
Views of outsiders	Anyone who doesn't conform is not allowed in.	?
View of wider society	Society is unfair. The state's institutions are unfriendly and unhelpful. Some of them, particularly the police and criminal justice system, are hostile, unjust and repressive.	?

| Role models and admired figures | Drawn from the worlds of popular culture, particularly music, style and fashion. Also sport, particularly football. Leaders of street gangs. Criminals. | ? |

The 'street culture' that Richardson and Wood characterise is not the only 'sub' or 'counter' culture that might influence how young people act and behave. In your group can you construct a third column from the perspective of an alternative youth (sub)-cultural community. For example, the BBC recently listed and described 14 different youth 'tribes' including 'sporties', 'plastics', 'moshers', 'campaigners' and 'hoodies' (**www.bbc.co.uk/ switch/them**).

Impacts of recent social change

Sociologists recognise that individuals – and perhaps young people in particular – also negotiate their identities and behaviour in relation to wider social, economic and political change. Relationships between 'culture', 'community' and 'identity' are becoming increasingly fragmented, fluid and complex. A number of changes have been particularly significant in destabilising social structures and the 'roles' performed (or expected) from different social groups. These include:

- the decline of traditional primary industries (such as coal mining and heavy manufacturing) and the creation of new kinds of employment with an emphasis on non-manual and service sector work;
- an increasing number of women entering the workforce;
- increasing variety in conceptions of 'normal' family life (i.e. increasing numbers of single-parent families, same-sex relationships;
- up until very recently, a period of sustained growth in the economy with an overall average increase in individual wealth;
- migration leading to increasingly diverse, multicultural communities;
- legal intervention to prevent discrimination in the workplace and public sector and to (attempt to) enshrine equality of opportunity.

A number of social theorists have characterised the contemporary period as one in which there is increased social mobility, that is, in which an individual's future is no longer determined by their socio-economic class background, their gender, or their race or ethnicity. Instead, their futures – and their identities – are about the choices they make and how effectively they can compete to take advantage of the opportunities provided to them by the twenty-first century. Echoing the earlier arguments of Talcott Parsons, success or failure is once again, often now presented as a private and personal responsibility.

For much of at least the last four decades, sociologists of education have concentrated their attention on complicating the picture of schooling and society offered by Talcott Parsons and others insisting that gender and race and class *do matter* as they impact individual's attitudes, behaviours and – perhaps most importantly – their opportunities. But is that sociological project now over? Have we managed to create a level playing field in which everyone is now free to be anybody and anything they want to be?

The most recent sociological evidence suggests that, yes, young peoples' identities are increasingly complex and cannot be reduced to just one dimension, be it 'gender' or 'race' or 'social class' (see for example Nayak and Kehily, 2008). However, research also documents that familiar inequalities *continue* to exist within schooling, and in some respects are actually being reinforced.

Primary school research by Reay and Wiliam (1999) documents that the recent increase in high-profile, high-stakes, standardised testing can have a profound and negative impact on children who now learn at a very young age to identify and value themselves primarily in terms of academic achievement and ability. *I'll be a nothing* reflects one ten year old in their study when contemplating failure in an upcoming SAT exam. Further research by Gillborn and Youdell (1999) also suggests that, when education becomes a competitive market place, the judgements of teachers become increasingly important as schools return to practices of streaming and selection in order to maximise their academic results. Gillborn and Youdell identify what they describe as a process of *educational triage*. They borrow their language from emergency medicine where 'triage' refers to quick decisions made by doctors on how to use limited resources to best effect. Here teachers consciously and unconsciously divide their students into three groups: those who are academically able ('safe' or 'healthy'); those who are 'treatable' and so deserving of attention; and those who are 'hopeless cases' with little chance of success. Critically, their research records that the interpretations teachers make of students' *potential* ability remain heavily influenced by expectations based on gender, class and ethnicity or race.

Perhaps even more tellingly, research by Beck *et al.* (2006) and Archer and Yamashita (2003) suggests that, by the time they reach their final year of compulsory schooling (aged 15/16), many young people have learned to *know their limits* (Archer and Yamashita, 2003) and opt for the 'safety' of stereotypically gender- and class-appropriate aspirations when making decisions about their futures after school (Beck *et al.*, 2006). Atkins (2008) provides an interesting addition to these arguments by exploring the classed and gendered nature of many young people's 'fantasy futures' of fame and fortune fed into by contemporary fixations with the culture of celebrity.

Reflective Task

At the 2008 conference of the Association for Teachers and Lecturers, it was reported that over 70 per cent of teachers surveyed believed that 'celebrity culture' was impacting students' aspirations for the future. The footballer/pop-star couple David and Victoria Beckham were considered by teachers to be male and female celebrities that students were most likely to model themselves on. Do you think that teachers would be likely to see the influence of 'celebrity culture' as a positive or negative thing? Why? How do you think celebrity culture might impact upon young people's understanding of gender, class and ethnic or racial roles?

Delegates at the conference were asked to debate and vote on a motion which argued that *the decline in this country into the cult of celebrity* is *perverting children's aspirations*. In pairs or small groups, recreate a similar debate.

Yet contemporary sociologists of education remain keen to remind us that it is important not to reduce our understanding of individuals to their membership of just one social group. These sociologists agree that the boundaries around groups built on gender, class and race or ethnicity are hard – perhaps impossible – to concretely define. They also ask that we do not forget that individuals *can* exercise agency: there is always the potential for dominant expectations to be resisted, subverted or changed. Their argument is that teachers and educational policy makers are wrong to assume that the school system is now – or has ever been – 'neutral' in terms of gender, class and race or ethnicity: socially constructed difference does continue to exist. However, they must equally be cautious not to wittingly or unwittingly reinforce difference. As Gaine and George reflect:

The willingness always to be surprised by pupils' work and potential is an important attribute in teachers, needing careful balancing with a knowledge of [and sensitivity to] generalisations derived from research.

Gaine and George, 1999, page 97

Chapter Summary

After reading this chapter, you should recognise that:

- In addition to transmitting common values, formal systems of education have a long history of reproducing differences between students from different social groups. As a consequence, schools (continue to) play an important role in reproducing social inequality.
- Examination of 'micro-level' classroom interaction can help us understand how wider social structures impact upon individuals' attitudes, behaviours and opportunities.
- Schools are not 'neutral' spaces: they are commonly shaped by the cultural expectations and values of the most powerful social groups.
- Official expectations for 'good behaviour' and 'academic success' are not the only demands that young people have to negotiate in constructing their own (learner) identities.

Research focus

Educational achievement and inequality

The discussions in this chapter can be framed by concerns over persistent inequalities in the academic achievement of different groups of students (as reflected in standardised examination results). Although published back in 2000, the following report still provides a useful starting point and exploratory analysis of apparent statistical trends:

- Gillborn, D and Mirza, HS (2000) *Educational inequality: mapping race, class and gender.* London: OFSTED.

What patterns and/or inconsistencies do the authors identify as especially significant? What dimension of identity appears to have the most consistent impact on examination success? Some may argue that certain groups of students are simply genetically cleverer or better than passing exams than others. What evidence do Gillborn and Mirza draw upon to undermine that claim?

You may also want to refer to the following texts to consider the dangers of relying too heavily on statistical data:

- Connolly, P (2006) Summary statistics, educational achievement gaps and the ecological fallacy. *Oxford Review of Education,* 32 (2): 235–52.

- Archer, L and Francis, B (2006) *Understanding minority ethnic achievement: race, gender, class and 'success'*. London: Routledge.

Intersections between gender, class and race or ethnicity

Increasingly, sociologists argue against looking at gender *or* class *or* race *or* ethnicity in isolation, and attempt to explore the ways that these aspects of identity intersect. For example, a number of writers have tried to show how expectations for 'male' behaviour vary by race or ethnicity and by social class. Choose two of the following texts. How many different ways of 'being masculine' or 'performing masculinity' do these writers identify? What do they mean by 'hegemonic masculinity'? And how might this be relevant for *all* students learning in schools?

- Archer, L (2003) *Race, masculinity and schooling*. Basingstoke: Open University Press.
- Connolly, P (2004) *Boys and schooling in the early years*. London: Routledge.
- Frosh, S, Phoenix, A and Pattman, R (2002) *Young masculinities: understanding boys in contemporary society*. Basingstoke: Palgrave.

Using theory to understand classroom interactions – Pierre Bourdieu

The theoretical discussions of Pierre Bourdieu have proven particularly popular and influential in recent sociological education research. This chapter described his use of the concept *cultural capital* but could also have explored the notions of 'field' and 'habitus'. Dianne Reay and Martin Grenfell provide useful discussion of how Bourdieu's ideas have and can be used:

- Reay, D (2004) 'It's all becoming a habitus': beyond the habitual use of habitus in educational research. *British Journal of Sociology of Education*, 25 (4): 431–44.
- Grenfell, M (2004) Bourdieu in the classroom, in Olssen M (ed) *Culture and learning: access and opportunity in the classroom*. Greenwich: Information Age.

You might also like to follow up by reading some of the research that Reay references in her article. Bourdieu described his concepts as 'thinking tools'. On the basis of your reading, do *you* find them useful in thinking about and making sense of schools?

Chapter 7

Learning and identity in a multicultural community

Learning outcomes

By the end of this chapter you should be able to:

- consider critically the ways in which the concept of culture has been used and is interpreted in contemporary educational debate;
- distinguish between multicultural (or pluralist) and monocultural (or assimilationist) educational approaches;
- recognise the historical, political and philosophical context of recent 'crisis Britishness' and 'education for national citizenships' debates;
- consider the forms of learning and knowledge required to equip students for cohesive citizenship in a multicultural community.

Chapter outline

If 'culture' is a complex and contested term, what does it mean in the context of a 'multi-cultural community', as contemporary Britain is regularly described? How is it understood and used by teachers and learners in contemporary British schools? This chapter argues that education systems in multicultural societies have two important and interrelated functions to perform:

- to strive for equality of opportunity and outcome between groups of students marked by ethnic, linguistic, national or religious diversity;
- to help all students respond positively when encountering such difference (for example, through fostering relationships of acceptance, understanding, empathy and respect).

It provides an historical discussion of multicultural education in Britain and demonstrates that the ignorance or denial of cultural difference can significantly disadvantage certain groups. However, over-reliance upon simplistic or 'essentialist' conceptions of cultural background can be just as damaging and it is important to critically examine the cultural explanations that are sometimes used to explain persistent patterns of educational inequality.

A national education system can also play an important role in communicating a sense of *common* culture: it has recently been argued that British schools must work harder to promote a sense of shared identity and citizenship. The chapter concludes by examining some of the problems and potential pitfalls of education for twenty-first century, multicultural 'Britishness'. In doing so, it attempts to provide a partial answer to questions posed earlier in the book; what, and *how*, is it most instructive for students to learn in a society that is increasingly characterised by diversity?

Education for the nation? Twenty-first century challenges

American children still begin their day at school by pledging allegiance to the flag, and that is why the Americans show a patriotism and a simple enthusiasm for their own country that our faded British sensibilities find childish.

Well, if you consider what is taught in British schools . . . it is hard to deny that in their assessment of what a nation needs to stick together, the Americans are right, and we are tragically wrong.

Boris Johnson, in the *Daily Telegraph*, July 2005

In recent years, the question of 'Britishness' – of people's sense of belonging to and identifying with the British nation or the national community – has been a recurring point of concern within popular and political debate. Much of this attention has focused upon what is being taught and learned in British schools. The reflections of Conservative politician Boris Johnson were written in response to the terrorist attacks on the London transport system in July 2005. Johnson was not the only commentator who interpreted the London bombings as a dramatic symptom of, amongst other things, a 'crisis' in British identity. Of particular concern was the fact that the men directly responsible were *home-grown* terrorists, *born and educated in Britain* (Howard, *The Guardian*, 2005). The country's schools, it was argued, had *failed to foster an adequate sense of belonging* in this generation of young men (Hinsliff, *The Observer*, 2005).

Of course, the motivations and catalysts behind such an act of terrorism are extremely complicated and not yet fully understood. But responses such as these are interesting and reflect a more general anxiety that contemporary British society – and contemporary British culture – is fragmenting and under attack.

It has been argued that 'multiculturalism' is bad for the health of the nation: too many different and incompatible cultures are being allowed to flourish, and those living in Britain are no longer adequately held together by common values or civic ties. There are challenges to be faced by formal education in holding together a plural, diverse and changing national society. Can a *shared* culture of national identification be created through compulsory schooling? At what cost to other, ethnic, religious or linguistic cultural identities? Must a community be 'stuck together' through cultural *sameness*? Or can schools equip young people with the skills and perspectives to respond to cultural *difference* more productively?

The discomfort of strangers: different sorts of difference and the threat to solidarity

In 2004, the journalist David Goodhart published an article entitled *The Discomfort of Strangers*. The piece provoked rather a lot of controversy but can usefully examined to understand the 'logic' of much recent anti-multicultural debate.

Goodhart's primary argument is that in a country such as Britain – which has relatively high levels of public expenditure on a well-developed welfare state – 'solidarity' between citizens depends upon individual members of society being able to imagine that the money they contribute through taxes, is likely to be spent on supporting other people sufficiently like themselves. He compared the situation of Scandinavian societies, characterised by high levels of ethnic and cultural similarity with popularly supported extensive social welfare systems, and the United States of America, marked instead by significant ethnic, racial and cultural diversity and with very limited provision of government-funded social support. Goodhart then went on to argue that perhaps there is a causal link: perhaps there are limits to the levels and forms of diversity that it is reasonable to expect citizens, and taxpayers to support?

Reflective Task

Think for a moment about some of the ways in which an individual might consider themselves 'like' or 'unlike' anyone else. Think of yourself among a group of students in a lecture hall. All of you are students, but who do you think you might share most in common with? Who do you perceive as most different from yourself? Why?

What about if you begin to consider friends and strangers outside of the lecture hall? Consider what you know – or might imagine – about some of the following people:

- a young British army recruit, currently serving in Afghanistan;
- a single mother bringing up two children on a part-time wage and income support and living on an inner-city council estate;
- a heroin addict;
- a convicted arsonist;
- a member of the landed gentry;
- a Rastafarian;
- a member of the British National Party;
- an anarchist;
- a political exile from Uganda;
- a footballer's wife whose husband earns over £50 000 a week during the football season and who can themselves charge large sums for a public appearance on reality TV.

Who do you believe you have most and least in common with? Who is most or least 'like you'? If you were (or are) a taxpayer, who do you feel you might least want your money to reach through the National Health Service, education system, state pension or Department for Social Support? Why? What forms of commonality and difference between people do *you* consider most important? Do you think other people in Britain would be likely to give the same answers? Why?

Given the variety of ways in which we could judge similarity and difference why do you think *cultural* diversity is so regularly presented as a key focus of concern?

What does it mean to live in a 'multicultural' society?

It has already been established that there are a number of possible dimensions to the concept of culture. Within the context of multiculturalism, most commentators are referring to a shared body of knowledge, beliefs and practices through which a group of people understand and identify themselves (after Parekh, 2002, page 2). Most often, the cultural groups referred to in 'multicultural' are also assumed to share a family-like heritage or history. This distinguishes them from other sorts of communities which are united instead by a common interest or shared circumstance, 'skater culture' for example, 'working class culture', or the 'boardroom culture' of business executives. In fact, the 'cultural' in multicultural is often used as a shorthand for what elsewhere might be characterised as the presence of different 'ethnic', 'racial', 'linguistic', 'national' and/or 'religious' groups (although, on occasion, you might come across 'multi-ethnic', 'multiracial' or 'multifaith' as more specific terms). And so 'Black British', 'Greek Cypriot', 'Muslim' and 'Gaelic', all currently function as labels for some of the communities spoken about in contemporary multicultural debate.

In its simplest sense, the word 'multicultural' is an adjective, used to describe the empirical reality that a particular society is made up of a population with more than one belief system, more than one language or religion and more than one 'traditional' way of life. 'Multicultural*ism*', however, refers to a set of specific philosophical, political and policy responses to that empirical fact.

Multiculturalism versus assimilationism?

A society can respond to cultural diversity in a number of different ways. It can celebrate and cherish it, respecting and/or offering protection to the distinct beliefs and traditions of cultural groups. Or it can perceive such diversity as a threat and attempt to reduce or entirely erase cultural difference in order to safeguard a single, homogenous way of life. This distinction will be reflected in a society's education system and its schools. The first response can be described as 'multiculturalist' or 'pluralist', the second as 'monoculturalist' or 'assimilationist'. Another way of characterising the distinction is to think of monoculturalism or assimilationism as a political philosophy which insists that to ensure equality of opportunity, every individual must be treated in exactly the same manner under the law. Multiculturalists on the other hand argue that, if we are to have any chance of realising equality – in terms of academic achievement, employment profile, or political representation, for example – concessions must be made to acknowledge people's differences.

Critical Thinking Task

Robin Richardson (2006) argues that, to ensure equality, educators should try to respond to difference among their pupils in a *discriminating* but not *discriminatory* way. Do you understand the distinction between the two terms? In partners or small groups, consider the following encounters or situations. In each case try to agree whether a *discriminating* or *discriminatory* decision has been made. Are the pupils described being treated fairly or unfairly? If you were in a position to make a decision, how would you respond?

- A group of pupils and one of their teachers decide to set up a lunch-time 'Asian girls' club at school. Individuals can come together to talk in a friendly and supportive atmosphere but *only* 'Asian girls' are allowed.
- Lansdowne School's uniform and personal appearance policy is very clear: no jewellery of any sort, no hats or headwear, boys' hairstyles must grow no longer than the bottom of their ears. On their first day at Lansdowne, the following students fall foul of the rules: Catherine, a white British Catholic wants to wear her crucifix to school; best friends Jason and Emmanuel both wear their hair in dreadlocks, Jason is white British with no religious faith whereas Emmanuel has been brought up Rastafarian; Fatima wants to wear her *hijab*; Tracy wears gold hoops in her ears.
- A university is starting a mentoring project with a local secondary school: mentors will be placed with all Year 7 students who are identified as belonging to an ethnic minority.

Multicultural Britain

Some empirical facts

In the year 2001, when the last census was published, approximately 8% of the British population considered themselves to belong to an ethnic minority. At least 11 different religions are practised (not including the various branches of Christianity) and it is estimated that 193 different languages are currently spoken in London alone. Britain is clearly a multicultural country in the first, descriptive, sense of the term. Indeed, in spite of nostalgic popular opinion to the contrary, a closer look at British history shows that this has always been the case.

Over five centuries, four, once independent, nations were brought together as one: remember, Wales has been linked with England since 1536 but the Act of Union between England and Scotland only took place in 1707; Ireland was incorporated in 1801 although the Republic of Ireland then gained independence in 1922. As Storry and Childs (2002) remind us, political unification has not necessarily led to cultural or social amalgamation, and in some important respects, the Welsh, the Scots and the Irish have retained identities and affiliations that distinguish them from each other and from the English majority. Indeed, at the close of the twentieth century, popular pressure led to the partial devolution of both Scotland and Wales with the creation of a Scottish Parliament and Welsh Assembly.

Britain has also long played host to both invited and uninvited settlers from across Northern Europe and the wider world: invading armies, persecuted refugees, enslaved labourers and economic migrants to name but a few. Given the tenor and tone of recent 'crisis Britishness' and 'Britain for the British!' debates, it is important to remember that:

- Black African people were first brought to Britain with the Roman army. Historical records suggest there has been a continuous Black population resident in Britain from the sixteenth century at least. Africans were also brought by force to these islands as slaves and servants throughout the seventeenth and eighteenth centuries;
- Jewish communities first arrived from France following the Norman conquests of 1066. Although violently expelled from the country in 1290 by King Edward I, their resettlement was permitted by Oliver Cromwell in 1656;
- the Islamic population in Britain – which comprise the focus of much most recent multicultural debate – dates back to at least the eighteenth century when Muslim sailors working on British merchant ships began to settle in port cities such as Cardiff, Glasgow, Liverpool and London.

However, the arrival of a boat, *The Empire Windrush*, at Tilbury in 1948 is seen to mark a significant turning point in Britain's social and demographic history. It was this period which precipitated the sort of popular and political discussions about how best to respond to cultural diversity which continue, enlivened, today.

Post-war migration and the failure of an early assimilationist approach

On board *The Empire Windrush* were just under 500 passengers arriving from the Caribbean; thousands more made the same journey in following years. These immigrants and later settlers from India, Pakistan and Bangladesh had been invited by the British government to address a severe labour shortage and to help rebuild the British economy following the Second World War. By the end of the 1960s, many British cities were home to firmly established African-Caribbean and South Asian communities. A 'second generation' of 'Black Britons' were being born here, growing up here and attending British schools. Originally, it had been hoped that these recent arrivals and their children would simply be absorbed – or 'assimilated' – into the wider community and British ways of life, but it soon become increasingly apparent that this was not to be the case. However, weaknesses in the country's economy and a shortage of desirable housing, contributed to a climate in which visible minorities in Britain were regularly met with hostility and/or suspicion and were not afforded the same opportunities as the rest of the population.

Assimilationism did not seem to be working: serious social and economic inequalities developed which created tensions between different groups; 1965 marked the first in a succession of pieces of 'race relations legislation' intended to ameliorate such inequality and avoid any future conflicts that might emerge. Minority communities argued forcefully that they would no longer be treated as second class citizens in structural or symbolic terms: they would not accept economic disadvantage or political disempowerment and they would no longer be represented or encountered with disrespect. And so, in the last decades of the twentieth century in Britain, a 'multiculturalism' – which recognised the rights of minority communities and affirmed their identities – was increasingly widely accepted as a more appropriate political response.

However, and as has already been seen, multiculturalism – as a political and a philosophical alternative to assimilationism – is not without critics of its own. Multicultural educational policy in particular has, since its inception, regularly been charged with the crimes of eroding British national identity and purposefully destroying national pride. Again, multiculturalism has become particularly vulnerable to criticism where it is perceived that the stability of wider society is under threat.

Reflective Task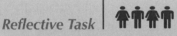

A report produced in 2000 by The Commission for the Future of Multi-Ethnic Britain highlighted seven recent trends which may have contributed to growing uncertainty and insecurity about British identity:

- post-World War Two immigration;
- globalisation;
- the long-term decline in Britain's position as a world power;
- the changing position of Britain in Europe;
- devolution of Scotland and Wales;
- the end of Empire;
- the rapid advance of social pluralism.

We have already referred to post-1948 immigration, but look over the six additional trends which have been identified. Are you confident you understand what each refers to? Do any require further explanation or detail? Are there any other trends or factors that you would like to add?

In small groups, or with a partner, consider which of the seven you consider is likely to have had the most significant effect. Try to justify your reasoning.

It is certainly true that in much popular and political discourse each of these trends is most often discussed in negative terms of challenge, disruption or potential threat. Imagine for a moment that you are a teacher of secondary school students and you are concerned to present an alternative point of view. Can you think of any ways you could discuss any (or all) of the same trends with your students but using instead a language of positive change and opportunity? Can you think of any ways they might also offer potential for enriching or transforming your practice as a teacher, or students' learning both inside and outside of schools?

Educational responses to cultural diversity

Monocultural curricula and the multiculturalist critique

Formal systems of education perform important roles in supporting both monocultural and multicultural models for society. If a national government is concerned with eliminating cultural difference and encouraging – or enforcing – assimilation, then education can be an extremely effective tool. It can reinforce the self-aggrandising belief systems of the powerful and disguise relationships of exploitation, oppression and dominance. Schools can present the particular norms and understandings of the dominant culture in society as though they are natural, universal and value-free. A monocultural curriculum would be particularly useful here. For example, a monocultural history curriculum could present its students with versions of the past which are partial, value-laden and told from a particular point of view. For many years, the history of the British Empire was presented in this fashion, as a story of 'the white man's burden' in 'civilising the savages'. The violent occupation of another people's land was explained in terms of Britons' 'natural' superiority and their political, economic and intellectual prowess in comparison with those who were colonised.

In fact, a common argument made by multiculturalist educators is that most traditional Western education is monocultural in this way. They suggest that curriculum materials are regularly extremely Eurocentric, positioning white (middle-class and male) Europeans at the height of human achievement – as the masters of science, the arts and political philosophy – and assuming that the world is being seen from a white (middle-class and male) point of view. Consider, for example, the implication of students being taught that Christopher Columbus 'discovered' America in 1492, or reading in a school text book that, during the 1750s, *not many people thought there was anything wrong with slavery* (reported in Richardson and Wood, 2000, page 41). Both statements render huge numbers of people completely invisible: as one Year 9 student astutely points out, in the second example, *the author* [of the text book] *is forgetting the slaves were* people *too* (Richardson and Wood, 2000, page 41, emphasis added).

Practical Task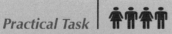

The Qualifications and Curriculum Authority has created a series of *Respect for All* web pages to help teachers explore the multicultural potential of all core and foundation subjects within the current national curriculum. These can be explored at the web address **www.qca.org.uk/qca_6753.aspx**.

Using the subject case studies provided online as a starting point, in small groups design a short lesson plan in each of the three core curriculum subject areas, English, maths and science and, if you have time, in one additional subject area. Try to make sure that your lessons reflect at least one dimension of good multicultural practice as identified by Nottingham City Schools in producing their Global and Anti-Racist Perspectives Pack.

- The cultural diversity of Britain and the world should be reflected.
- Students should be shown that the achievements of individuals and cultures are universal and not only Western.
- Students should be helped to talk about and challenge unfair generalisations and racism as well as to examine prejudices and different perspectives.

The hidden curriculum

It is not only through the official curriculum and teaching materials that an assimilationist or multiculturalist logic can be transmitted through schools. Again, schools transmit expectations of 'normal' and legitimate behaviour in a number of less explicit ways. The manner in which a student's home language is valued or undermined, for example, can be read as a reflection of wider policy and political perspectives as to how (and whether) they should be integrated into society (Leung, 2001; see also Rattansi, 1992, discussed below). Schools as public spaces can permit or prohibit other signs of cultural difference too. In France, for example, where the national government has for many years adopted a very clear and strong principle of cultural assimilation and neutral, civic, national citizenship, there has been considerable controversy surrounding attempts made by a number of young French, female, Islamic students to wear visible symbols of their faith to school.

Official British education rsponse

Minority cultures as an 'obstacle' to learning

With regard to the British experience, throughout the 1950s and early 1960s, the main thrust of educational policy towards cultural diversity was very definitely assimilationist. As a report from the Commonwealth Immigration Advisory Committee made clear, it was believed that:

A national system of education must aim at producing citizens in a society properly equipped to exercise rights and perform duties which are the same as other citizens. If their parents were brought up in another culture or another tradition, children should be encouraged to respect it, but a national system cannot be expected to perpetuate the different values of immigrant groups.

Commonwealth Immigration Advisory Committee, 1964, page 7

The message here is that even where alternative cultures might be 'respected', their subservience to the values and rights of the majority is not to be called into question. A number of commentators have highlighted that in Britain, early educational policy interventions directed towards the children of recent immigrants were motivated as much by the need to assuage and reassure white parents as by concerns over the educational opportunities of the minority pupils themselves (Tomlinson, 1983). The first major intervention from the Department for Education and Science was the production of a pamphlet entitled *English for Immigrants* in 1963. Students who arrived in Britain with no or little knowledge of English were pressurised to adopt the language as their primary method of communication as quickly as possible in order that they did not present such a challenge to their teachers and fellow classmates at school. Ali Rattansi has argued that here, the teaching of English was a metaphor for a broader policy of enforced assimilation and that this reflected the popular view:

that 'immigrant' cultures – the desire to hold on to which was seen as evidence of a 'ghetto mentality' – were an educational hindrance requiring vigilant exclusion from the culture of the school.

Rattansi, 1992, page 15

Schools were also given special financial assistance if they were attended by significant numbers of pupils who spoke a foreign language or came from unfamiliar cultural backgrounds. A policy of 'dispersal' was also advocated which meant the bussing of African-Caribbean and Asian students outside of their immediate catchment area in order that they did not become over-represented within any one particular school. In these ways, 'culture' – or at least the culture of certain groups of students – was positioned very clearly as a problem, an 'educational hindrance' in Rattansi's words. At the same time, this model of educational philosophy appears also to suggest that a student's cultural background was something which could, if necessary, be forgotten, ignored or denied: a shackle that the right sort of schooling could overcome.

As the 1960s drew to a close, politicians and educationalists were caused to consider that perhaps this was not the case. Again, immigrant communities had not 'assimilated' in the manner that had been expected and this became especially apparent in the continued educational underperformance of certain groups of students in schools. Recognising that their children's educational success or failure had key consequence for their later opportunity and potential mobility in life, the growing disenchantment and frustration of ethnic minority parents crystallised around inequality and disadvantage in schools. In order to prevent their further alienation, and to avoid potential ensuing confrontation, a change in strategy in educational policy needed to be pursued.

Again, assimilationist rhetoric began to be replaced by a language that introduced the idea that 'equal opportunities' might only be realised through the recognition of certain sorts of difference. At this juncture, 'difference' was framed primarily in terms of 'special assistance' or 'special need' (Rex, 1989). In a 1969 report written by the Select Committee on Race Relations and Immigration (SCCRI), it was identified that young Black Britons were among those requiring such special assistance in a comparable manner to *backward school children* and the *physically handicapped* (SCRRI, 1969, page 31). While there is arguably something potentially progressive in the suggestion that particular attention should be focused upon the disadvantage experienced by certain groups of young people, the characterisation of an ethnic identity as a 'handicap' is very problematic indeed. Although, it was no longer suggested that a student's culture could or should be ignored by the educational system, the understanding that 'home cultures' could comprise a primary obstacle to educational achievement remained firmly in place.

Explaining academic failure and success

Throughout the 1970s, there was growing awareness of the apparent pattern that 'Asian' (in fact, primarily Indian) students were beginning to perform especially successfully in British schools but that African-Caribbean (then referred to as 'West Indian') students continued to lag behind. This only served to fuel the logic of 'culture as obstacle' further still. Attempts to understand the pattern were clear in where they believed the explanation could be found: *the reasons for the very different school performances of Asians and West Indians seem likely to lie within their respective cultures*, argued the high-profile and influential 1985 Swann Report (page 87). For Swann and numerous other social scientists and policy makers, 'Asian' pupils, were:

given to 'keeping their heads down' and adopting a 'low profile', thereby making it easier to succeed in a hostile environment. West Indians, by contrast, are given to 'protest' and 'a high profile' with the reverse effect.

Swann Report, 1985, page 86

Likewise, the Asian community was characterised as 'tight-knit', respectful and supportive, while the African-Caribbean community, in keeping with much value-laden and Western-centric social and policy research of the time, was framed in terms of broken family structures, female-headed households, disrespect, irreverence and impoverishment (Centre for Contemporary Cultural Studies, 1982). In this way African-Caribbean culture was effectively 'pathologised' as deviant and/or deficient, in comparison to both Indian culture and dominant Western norms.

The Swann Report did represent a significant advance on earlier official policy discussion because, for the first time, it fully acknowledged that the education system was itself not without fault. The short quotation presented above does after all make the important recognition that British schools, and British society as a whole, might comprise a 'hostile environment' from the vantage point of an ethnic minority child. However, by relying upon familiar, 'commonsense' and 'culturalist' explanations for student success rates, attention was all too easily diverted away from broader structures of institutional and societal racism. It was these which had contributed to producing hostility in the first place, yet in Swann and others' formulations it is the African-Caribbean students themselves – through their culturally sanctioned but inappropriate and unhelpful responses to hostility – who are once again positioned as responsible for their own disadvantage in schools.

In attempting to explain student achievement, both then and now, it is important not to treat culture as though it can be examined independently from other dynamics that might be at work. There are in fact a number of potential explanations for why Indian students in British schools continue to appear to do better than their African-Caribbean counterparts. For example, evidence suggests that the Indian heritage population in Britain tends to be concentrated in higher socio-economic classes, and social class remains another key contributor to educational failure or success. Likewise, the parents of Indian pupils tend themselves to have been educated to a higher level than the parents of African-Caribbean students, and more Indian students are enrolled in fee-paying and selective schools. The Swann Report failed to explore any of these possibly explanatory facts.

Ethnic monitoring and 'strategic essentialisms'

It is now a statutory obligation for schools to collect and record information for all their students on the basis of 'ethnic' identity. This measure was intended to prevent particular groups from being disadvantaged by making persistent inequalities in educational outcome and experience transparently clear. Most commentators recognise that such ethnic labels are themselves problematic and rather limited but argue that they currently function as a necessary evil – a 'strategic essentialism' – without which it would be impossible to identify examples of good practice, or highlight areas of particular concern (Modood *et al.* 2002). In fact, this sort of measurement reflects a broader trend, which has encouraged ethnic monitoring in analysis of many different aspects of day-to-day life.

Practical Task

Can you think of the last time you were asked to make a note of your cultural background or ethnicity? Did you consider the question appropriate? And how easy did you find this to do?

Visit your nearest library and try to find a recent volume of a publication like *Social Trends*. How easy is it to find statistics broken down by ethnicity? Can you locate yourself within one of the ethnic labels used? How meaningful do you consider this label? What do you think it tells us about you? What does it fail to capture? How might it be useful in describing or explaining your own experiences at school?

None of the arguments presented above are intended to suggest that it is at all helpful to ignore or deny a student's cultural heritage. Educational success continues to comprise a key predictor of social and economic opportunity. It is therefore absolutely necessary for schools and the education system to equip all students fairly if we are to have any hope of realising a socially just society.

Recent research has offered some suggestion that a student's cultural background *might* result in educationally significant variations in, amongst other things; their preference for collaborative and/or communal as opposed to individualistic and/or competitive learning styles; the emphasis placed upon and meaning attached to 'educational success', whether in purely instrumental or broader terms; their response to and understanding of contextualised humour, idiom and/or other verbal and non-verbal communication codes (Irvine and York, 1995). An educator entirely unaware of such possible variation might misinterpret certain student responses in terms of recalcitrance, disinterest or lack of ability, with potentially damaging consequences for the learning experience of the child. Therefore, treating all students in exactly the same manner is not necessarily the best way to ensure equality of outcome or opportunity. However, it is crucially important to recognise, as most research goes on to suggest, that variation *within* a single cultural group is often just as significant (if not more so) than overall patterns of variation *between*. However, if we are looking for differences between groups, this is what we are more likely to see.

Paul Connolly (2006) warns strongly against the uncritical acceptance of group-level generalisations drawn from crude statistics being applied to individual students in schools. One of the many contradictions of the contemporary period is that, while people's lives, identities and experiences are becoming more complex and unpredictable, the mass media and our politicians increasingly want to present information as though it is simple, fixed and clear. In education this is reflected in the regular circulation of attention-grabbing, but often rather misleading, headline figures which report 'achievement gaps' between aggregated groups. This can prevent a more critical and sophisticated analysis able to recognise that there is significant overlap *between* students from different cultural backgrounds. It ignores the impact of other dimensions of identity such as gender or social class and pays no attention to the influence of good – and bad – practice in different schools.

The important point is that we must remain especially careful and critical about the notions of culture – and for that matter of all other forms of 'grouped difference' – that we work with and attempt to understand. This is true of multicultural education as a whole, even where a student's cultural background is presented not as an educational 'obstacle' but as a source of pride.

Recognising difference and celebrating diversity

One of the most popular and widely adopted forms of multicultural intervention which developed as a response to the critiques of monocultural curricula described above was built around what is known more broadly in political philosophy as *the politics of recognition* (Taylor, 1994). If monocultural and Eurocentric curricular content and teaching materials had ignored or devalued the experience and perspective of minority communities, then a multicultural curriculum should demand their recognition and celebration in schools. And so, from the 1970s onwards, teachers and local education authorities have been actively encouraged to positively and publicly engage with the home cultures of students at their schools. 'Multicultural events', where students are invited to bring in significant cultural artefacts, wear 'traditional' clothing or prepare 'traditional' food, are illustrative of this approach.

But here there is an additional danger: of 'tokenism' and of capturing cultures in a rather shallow and artificially frozen pose. Contemporary social theory considers all cultures to be fluid, dynamic and the site of ongoing renegotiation and internal contest. But all of this is rather hard to communicate in the classroom. It appears a lot easier to present a snap-shot simplification of symbols of cultural difference, of *saris, samosas and steel-bands* as Barry Troyna once famously criticised (Troyna and Williams, 1985). Where minority cultures are presented for educational consumption, it is important to ask, who gets to decide how a particular cultural identity is characterised? Are all members of a community likely to see their shared culture in precisely the same way? If not, whose versions are we most likely to see and hear?

Treating all cultures as something to be uncritically 'respected' in their entirety is also problematic, because 'culture' and 'tradition' can be called upon to defend practices which not everybody considers acceptable or fair. Arguably fox hunting is part of British cultural heritage but is something that many Britons are fiercely critical of, so much so that in 2005 it was criminalised. Sometimes 'respect' for other people's cultures can translate into a fear of appearing in anyway critical, or turn into a 'cultural relativism' whereby anything goes. Heidi Safia Mirza (2008) argues that this is a dangerous position and an inappropriate one for teachers to take. She suggests that:

The privileged position and intellectual status teachers enjoy carry an obligation to be aware of and respond to abuses suffered by their students.

Mirza, 2008, page 2

Mirza uses the example of young girls being forced against their will into arranged marriages to argue that sensitivity to cultural and community traditions should not be considered more important than ensuring individual's human rights. In fact, the challenge of balancing respect for individual and cultural group rights remains very contentious and lies right at the heart of multicultural politics (Parekh, 2002).

No single cultural perspective has the moral or intellectual high-ground; each should be open to scrutiny and possible contestation and each should be given the opportunity to develop and change. In schools and other educational spaces, cultural difference should not be rendered invisible or undermined but nor should it be caricatured, over-simplified, or reified. The conceptions of culture that we work with and learn with matter; limited understandings of culture can result in limited understandings of relationships *across* cultures and across difference.

'What about us?' 'White backlash' and the teaching of Britishness

'I do feel sometimes that there is no white history. There's either Black History Month or they do Muslims and Sikhs. We learn about that but we don't learn about white people, so we do feel a bit left out as well.

Reported in Ajegbo, 2007, page 30

If minority cultures have been regularly presented as though they can be clearly identified and singled out for celebration in classrooms, then it is perhaps not too surprising that there has been a growing chorus of 'majority' voices asking: 'Why isn't it the same for us?'; 'Where is our culture in these multicultural models?'; 'Why (and by whom) has our culture been taken away?'; and 'Why aren't we allowed to talk and learn about our own culture, in our own country, in our schools?'.

Unfortunately, few educational approaches have made any serious attempt to answer or constructively engage with questions such as these. As a consequence, research from the early 1980s onwards has regularly documented the growing frustration of significant numbers of 'white' pupils, their confusion over the nature and status of their own identities and their alienation from, or out-and-out rejection of, multiculturalist ideas and debate (Troyna and Hatcher, 1992; Gillborn, 1995). Similar findings were recorded in the Ajegbo Report, published in early 2007 and interpreted in popular and media discourse to warn that *White students need sense of culture* (*Birmingham Post*, 25 January 2007), and *White pupils 'losing their identity'* (*The Daily Mail* 25 January 2007).

One response to these claims would be to attempt to provide students with what they appear to be asking for: for schools to attempt to document, resurrect or champion the history, customs and traditions of 'Britishness' (and/or) 'whiteness' as the culture of the majority. But recent experience suggests that deciphering a shared and agreed-upon understanding of what comprises British culture (let alone 'whiteness') is an impossibly difficult task. Do you think it is something that you would be able to do?

Perhaps more importantly, to attempt it would only serve to reinforce the problematic notion that cultures really can be presented as singular and stable things. Perhaps the sense of unfairness that many young white students appear to consider they are facing is not really the function of unfairness at all. Perhaps the perception that *majority culture* appears to be nowhere depends upon a failure to recognise (or to have been made aware of) the fact that majority cultural expectations, norms and values continue to be present almost everywhere. Are white people really being 'left out' of a school curriculum which clearly signposts 'Black History', and 'does Muslims and Sikhs'? Or is such signposting only glaringly apparent in comparison to the implicit presence of whiteness throughout the entire rest of the curriculum? Perhaps only unless otherwise specified, the default position for the rest of the history taught in schools continues to be the history of white Kings and Queens, white generals and soldiers and white politicians, spokesmen, artists and scientists.

The Ajegbo report suggested that there should be a renewed emphasis on British identity, British history and core British values within schools. But there is considerable cause for concern if this renewed emphasis presents a history and identity that is uncritically celebrated or artificially simplified. The 'British values' that Ajegbo and many contemporary politicians want to champion are things like 'tolerance', 'respect', 'justice' and 'democracy'. Certainly there is much scope for teachers and their students to explore these through discussion of the establishment of parliament, equal rights legislation and the rule of law. But we must remember that contemporary Britain is also built on histories of slavery, colonialism, persecution and exploitation. Like *all national histories*, it is a history of contradiction and competing impulses: of 'progress' through 'reason' and scientific rationality as well as enduring structural inequality and prejudice.

As Richardson and Miles summarise:

It is important that children throughout Britain should be helped to make sense of the muddle that history has bequeathed to them. Muddle can be confusing and dispiriting – but can also be consoling and exhilarating. Children need to understand that Britishness is not something fixed and final but has always been contested; that it has evolved and changed over the centuries; and that it is evolving still.

Richardson and Miles, 2003, page 57

Learning for contemporary (multi)culture

An important educational distinction can be made between treating culture (whether an overarching 'British culture' or any of the multiple other cultures from which British society is made) as either:

- a set of fixed practices, products and/or values; or
- a *process*, which is always ongoing, always open to contest and always open to change.

Learning in contemporary (multi)culture should be about equipping young people to recognise themselves as agents of cultural production and change. It should also be about encouraging students to encounter difference as an opportunity for learning and for dialogue. 'Respect' for cultural difference should entail recognition that *all* cultures are multi-dimensional and open to contest. Schools also have a responsibility here to help students recognise and challenge their own and other people's prejudice. However, this is not always an easy or comfortable task. It depends upon schools and classrooms being (or becoming) environments where people feel able to ask difficult questions and do not feel threatened if it is not possible to come up with one concrete answer. It needs students and teachers to develop critical thinking and empathetic listening skills and it asks that people remain open to the multiple ways that they can learn from each other while recognising that *we all* speak from and see things from a partial point of view.

Richardson and Wood provide very useful advice for educators when they remind us that all individuals make choices amongst and within the cultures they are born with and those others in which they may take part. Schools have an important role to play in supporting and guiding young people through the choices they make. Schools should help ensure that a person's identity is:

- *confident, strong and self-affirming, as distinct from uncertain, ashamed or insecure;*
- *open to change, choice and development, as distinct from being unreflective, doctrinaire and rigid;*
- *receptive and generous towards other identities, and prepared to learn from them, as distinct from feeling threatened and hostile, and wishing to exclude or to be separate.*

Richardson and Wood, 2000, page 25, after Runnymede Trust 1993

Critically, a person's identity is not reducible to just their cultural heritage (or heritages). A person's identity is also built on their relationships with other people. A person who is feeling confident, strong and secure in their position in society, or within the classroom, is less likely to feel threatened or hostile when encountering difference than one who is already feeling undermined, uncertain and/or insecure.

Chapter Summary

After reading this chapter, you should recognise that:

- The recent 'crisis Britishness' debates which have impacted upon education depend upon a very partial reading of British history which fails to recognise that there have always been disparate cultural communities living in the British Isles.
- The last 60 years of British educational policy and practice have seen a number of problematic understandings of the home cultures of students from immigrant communities. These have been: purposefully ignored and denied value or significance; interpreted as an 'obstacle' to learning or as a 'handicap'; crudely simplified and subject to over-generalisation; presented as something fixed and firm; and reified as something that people are anxious not to appear to criticise.
- If we understand that all cultures are fluid, changing and internally contested, then learning for multicultural citizenship should be concerned with helping students negotiate and critically evaluate existing cultural formations as well producing new cultural forms of their own.

Research focus

Background

Audrey Osler provides a useful commentary on the 2007 Ajegbo Report and relates it to wider political and philosophical discussion of multiculturalism, identity and difference. Can you identify what she considers to be the strengths and limitations of the report?

- Osler, A (2008) 'Citizenship education and the Ajegbo report: re-imagining a cosmopolitan nation'. *London Review of Education*, 6 (1): 11–25.

Identity rights

Kathleen Hall explores the relationships and possible tensions between cultural identity and individual human rights with reference to the lives and experiences of young British Sikhs.

- Hall, K (1995) 'There's a time to act English and a time to act Indian': the politics of identity among British-Sikh teenagers, in Stephens, S (ed) *Children and the politics of culture.* Chichester: Princeton University Press.

She uses an important quote from Veena Das to argue that:

It is not only the right to cultural identity [that is important] but also to cultural innovation, play with other identities, availability of the whole repertoire of the culture of man and woman which is the heritage of the child.

Hall, page 244

What is the implication for teachers from Hall's study? How can they ensure that a child's right to 'cultural innovation' and to 'play' with multiple identities is protected in schools?

Teacher training

Teachers clearly have a very important role to play in facilitating potentially difficult discussion about difference and cultural identity. What particular competencies, understandings and skills do teachers need to do this and what support and assistance is available to them? The following book is based on research with trainee teachers;

• Jones, R (1999) *Teaching racism or tackling it? Multicultural stories from white beginning teachers*. Stoke on Trent: Trentham.

In Chapter 7, Jones presents 36 statements reflecting views held by trainee and/or established teachers from his research. He considers each to be problematic. Can you explain why? How commonly do you think each of these perspectives is held and how can they be addressed?

Chapter 8

Outside the school gate:
alternative cultures of learning

Learning outcomes

By the end of this chapter you should be able to:

- identify and evaluate ways that the culture of formal schooling might impair positive learning experiences;
- outline and assess a range of theories and practices that offer alternative cultures of learning (Freire, unschooling, Steiner);
- consider the possibilities and threats for learning by advances in technology;
- reflect on the extent that formal schooling can and does make use of alternatives like those outlined in the chapter to foster more engaging cultures of learning.

Chapter outline

While educational counter-cultures in the UK may have peaked in the 1970s, there are still important movements worthy of consideration. Contemporary cultural sentiments of blame, cynicism and fear mean that the authority of mainstream education continues to be questioned and alternatives are reasserted, revised and articulated. Today, there are numerous learning spaces existing outside the formal education setting. And arguably, recent changes in culture and technology provide a growing number of opportunities for alternatives to develop.

In particular, a growing emphasis on community has resulted in a boom in the number of localised, informal and grass-roots educational projects. The emergence of new technologies provides opportunities for very different learning spaces to be constructed. As the notion of educational choice becomes increasingly prevalent, alternative forms of schooling are becoming more and more high profile and popular. Many of these alternatives have small but vociferous support, frequently attracting fervent disciples and cult-like status.

We must move away from a view of education as a rite of passage involving the acquisition of enough knowledge and qualifications to acquire an adult station in life. The point of education should not be to inculcate a body of knowledge, but to develop capabilities: the basic ones of literacy and numeracy as well as the capability to act responsibly towards others, to take initiative and to work creatively and collaboratively. The most important capability, and the one which traditional education is worst at creating, is the ability and yearning to carry on learning. Too much schooling kills off a desire to learn . . .

Leadbeater, 2000, page 226

Of course, it is too easy to offer a one-sided and overly pessimistic account of schooling: formal education is no 'sociopath'. Teachers do not set out with the aim of crushing the inquisitive nature of young children. In fact, the opposite is almost universally true – that teachers become teachers because they are stimulated by the qualities that young people possess and because they recognise the value of their role in nurturing effective learners. Nevertheless, it is also true that many young people become disillusioned and detached from learning as a result of their schooling experiences.

The chapter questions the extent that formal education can learn from and/or adapt to the multiple forms and settings that learning takes place in today. It asks how far these alternative educational cultures contribute to (complement or contradict) our understanding of learning today. It identifies principles and strategies that formal schooling already 'borrows from' these alternatives, identifying two substantial areas:

- e-learning and electronic cultures of learning;
- community education and informal learning.

Finally, based on material covered during the chapter, it offers a radically alternative culture of learning for the future.

What's wrong with formal schooling?

Despite recent rhetoric concerning 'choice' and 'personalised learning', it is hard to get away from the idea that the structure of formal schooling promotes a 'one size fits all' culture of learning. The education system and national curriculum define what children and young people learn, what levels of achievement are appropriate for each stage of development, where learning takes place and how and by whom learning is assessed – it is worth noting that the new 'early years foundation stage' extends this control to include children before they attend school.

Many educationalists have expressed concern at the conception of learning that is cultivated within schools. For instance, in his highly influential book *Deschooling society*, Ivan Illich argued that professional control over learning results in a profoundly distorted realisation of learning. The pupil, he argued, is *'schooled' to confuse teaching with learning, grade advancement with education, a diploma with competence, and fluency with the ability to say something new* (Illich, 1973, page 9). Schools maintain a myth (accepted by pupils and teachers alike) that learning equates to being taught, and that grades and certificates are indistinguishable from successful learning. The capacity to express an idea in a convincing and 'academic' style can be more valued than that of originality and independence of thought. For Illich, and those influenced by his ideas, the 'ownership' of legitimate learning by educational professionals (concentrated within the confines of formal educational institutions) results in a culture of learning that is inauthentic and disempowering to pupils. Genuine learner engagement is undermined by compulsory schooling that takes place in certain places at certain times and under the guidance of a particular group defined as 'experts'.

The massive expansion and extension of surveillance systems within formal education might further impoverish the culture of learning. Monitoring instruments include repeated examination, formal and informal (and external and internal) inspection and observation, and a rapid growth in management information systems. These contribute to a culture where all participants are being (and *feel* like they are being) monitored all of the time. Drawing from the seminal work of Michel Foucault (1991), who equated schools with prisons in a *disciplinary society*, critics claim that formal schooling is now characterised by surveillance and that the visibility of surveillance data puts tremendous pressure on everyone involved. For example, Wrigley (2006) cites the advent of 'high stakes testing', particularly publicised league tables and performance-related pay, as crucial in the reshaping of learning and teaching. Wrigley

Reflective Task

Consider how far your experiences of formal schooling coincide with the negative accounts that you have encountered in this section. To help with this, read John Taylor Gatto's *Seven lesson schoolteacher* (2002). You can find it at **http://www.informationliberation. com/?id=11375**. Written from his experiences as a school teacher, Gatto claims children learn seven detrimental lessons from their schooling. Complete Table 8.1:

Table 8.1 Seven detrimental lessons from schooling. Adapted from Gatto (2002)

	Summarise Gatto's claim	Your example	Your argument against Gatto
Confusion			
Class position			
Indifference			
Emotional dependency			
Intellectual dependency			
Provisional self-esteem			
One can't hide			

Now consider the following from your own experiences of schooling.

- Potentially damaging impacts that formal schooling has on children.
- What do you see as the benefits of formal schooling?
- How do you view the criticisms of formal schooling that have been raised in this section in terms of your own learning experiences?
- Would you consider an alternative for your children – why?

persuasively argues that educational policy with roots in the 1980s has had a corrosive effect on school culture and has *systematically trivialised* (2006, page 24) learning within formal education. Distorting effects include:

- teachers' overriding priority is test preparation;
- coaching pupils to desired answers, and guilt if not linking teaching directly to exams;
- increasing bureaucracy and information systems having a massive burden on teachers' time;
- all learning activity needs to be 'on paper' and measurable in 'performance indicators';
- a homogenisation/standardisation of teaching strategies and subject content;
- students and teachers as individuals who are mistrustful of one another.

Learning outside formal schooling

The following section will reflect the heterogeneity of contemporary cultures of learning by examining a range of alternatives. These are discussed as:

- alternative theories of learning and culture: AS Neill and Paulo Freire, critical pedagogy – especially the ideas of self-governance and 'culture circles';
- alternatives to schooling: unschooling and 'free skooling' – learning without schooling;
- alternative forms of schooling: Montessori and Steiner – learning in different types of school.

Neill, Freire and critical pedagogy

Two 'cultural' critiques of schooling have been especially significant in shaping alternative visions of learning today. The theorisations of AS Neill (1883–1973) and Paulo Freire (1921–1997) both build from a critique of formal schooling to offer radical alternatives, constructing what they regard as positive cultures of learning. While Neill's ideas draw from a liberal education tradition, those of Freire are influenced by Marxist analysis.

Neill, a Scottish progressive educator, viewed the society he lived in as predominantly unhappy and hate-filled. He saw the roots of these problems in formal schooling. For Neill, mainstream schooling was based on an adult perception of childhood, dictated by the anxiety of parents. He argued too much emphasis was placed on reason, at the expense of social and emotional development. Formal education imposed constraints on the child, measured success by academic achievement and did not allow children the freedom and space to develop. The result of such a system was repressed, subservient and unhappy children (Neill, 1970).

Neill's alternative educational philosophy was based on the following beliefs (Vaughan, 2006):

- an optimistic viewpoint on childhood – *a child is innately wise and realistic*;
- centrality of (child) happiness (inner wellbeing, contentment, balance);
- real interest/learning comes from within, not from compulsion, punishments or rewards;
- freedom – *a free range childhood* (but not licence to do harm to others);
- education should result in self-regulating individual and community persons – self-regulation principle.

Neill put these principles into practice by setting up an independent boarding school, Summerhill, in 1921. It is still going strong today. The school is built on democratic values. It is run by a school meeting in which everyone has an equal voice. Decisions are made collectively and implemented by the head, Neill's daughter Zoe. There is no compulsion to attend classes and there are no school years. Pupils are encouraged to make their own art (plays, music, paintings).

Perhaps the most influential contemporary educational 'radical' is Paulo Freire. Freire conceived of education both as the instrument by which the powerful maintain an unequal social order and as the means through which such inequalities could be challenged and dismantled. As such, education is not and cannot be neutral. Teachers either support the status quo (and therefore the oppressors) or fight for change (for the oppressed):

Education either functions as an instrument which is used to facilitate integration of the younger generation into the logic of the present system and bring about conformity or it becomes the 'practice of freedom', the means by which men and women deal critically and creatively with reality and discover how to participate in the transformation of their world.

Freire and Macedo, 2000, page 34

For Freire, formal schooling creates people who are 'captives of their ignorance': who are unable to conceive of alternatives to the inequality and oppression that characterises contemporary society. Freire terms the existing culture of learning in formal schooling 'banking education', claiming that learners are conceived of as little more than 'receptacles'. Their passive role is to receive, file and store deposits of information (Freire and Macedo, 2000, page 73). This 'jug-and-mug' education shapes the learner to be an observer of the world as it is, rather than as a social actor who has the capacities to change it.

Freire argues for a *liberatory* or *problem-posing* education, where the teacher is motivated by a commitment to the oppressed. The main principles of this alternative include:

- teachers and students as simultaneously teachers and students ('teacher-students' and 'student-teachers');
- teacher and student as critical co-investigators who have joint responsibility for learning;
- learning and thinking take place through communication and dialogue;
- education as a process of 'mutual humanisation', whereby learning takes place in authentic relations and where real-life injustices and inequities are at the heart of the learning experience;
- *praxis* – there must be a clear relationship between learning and practical application;
- raising *critical consciousness* to equip learners with the desires and skills to transform the world.

Central to Freire's *problem-posing* education is the use of *culture circles* as a teaching method: whereby learners use their own ways of speaking to articulate a shared understanding of their social reality and to devise ways of acting in order to change their future (Freire, 2005). This alternative version of education provided the theoretical foundation for *critical pedagogy* (Giroux, 1988). This current theory has taken Freire's ideas and applied them to all oppressed groups, identifying a range of teaching strategies to sustain learner empowerment.

While Neill and Freire approached learning from very different political starting points, they both developed conceptions of education that place the learner categorically at the centre of the process. They both perceive the role of education to be fostering a culture in which learning equates the development of critical engagement, independence of mind and autonomy. And they both view congruence in the role of the learner and the teacher as an essential prerequisite. Although it is difficult to conceive of an entire educational system based on these principles, their ideas have proved highly influential.

Unschooling and 'free skooling'

Unschooling is a version of home schooling that developed out of the work of John Holt (1997). Influenced by Neill's work, Holt argued that schools are not healthy places to grow up in. He claimed that children are confused by a schooling system that imposes a fragmented and content-heavy curriculum onto them. Inhibited by a fear failure, the child becomes intellectually and emotionally dependent on their teachers. The worst effect of these and other schooling factors, according to Holt, is that children lose their natural desire to learn (Holt, 1990).

In unschooling, learning takes place outside of formal schooling. Parents facilitate their child's learning, but it is the child who essentially directs her own learning. Making the most of natural inquisitiveness, the child decides for herself what, how, where and when she learns. The parent facilitates learning by providing opportunities and frameworks in accordance with the child's interest on a given day. There are no externally defined curriculum: no set of subjects, no dates, no exams, no compulsion. The focus is not on the content but on the process of learning. From the perspective of the unschooler, if children maintain a love of learning, they will always want to do it.

Especially in the USA, there are a growing number of networks and support centres for unschoolers to make use of and to meet one another. One example is the 'Not Back to School Camp' (NBTSC) for unschooled teenagers. Week-long meetings are arranged in which young people:

swim; talk; sing; drum; dance; hike; stare at the sky; play volleyball and softball and soccer; make nifty things in crafty workshops; take creative, emotional, and intellectual risks; encourage each other to do amazing things; have talent shows; teach and learn from each other.

NBTSC, 2008

As these networks develop and grow in number, the emphasis shifts from the parent having the time, skill and finance to appropriately facilitate their child's learning.

Of course, the notion of unschooling is rather extreme and is open to heavy criticism, on both theoretical and practical grounds. Critics question whether children are capable of deciding for themselves what they should learn. Children's development might be hindered by a lack of exposure to different cultures and the lack of opportunities to develop interaction and other social skills – it can sound pretty lonely and relies heavily on the time and skills of parents. It is also difficult to see how unschooled children can achieve certification for their educational achievements in the same way that 'schooled' children can. Most would claim that children are better off learning in the regulated and safe environment of a formal institution, with trained and certified 'experts' looking after them.

Free schooling (or 'free skooling') is closely related to unschooling. In fact, organisations like 'Not Back to School Camp' blur the boundaries between unschooling and 'free skooling'. Although the origins were in anarchist schools in Spain in the early twentieth century, like unschooling, 'free skools' are at their most developed in the USA today. 'Free skools' are informal networks of adults and children acting collectively to create educational opportunities and skill sharing within their communities. In all instances, the distinction between teacher and learner is minimal and all workshops are voluntary.

There is a wide range of educational activities that come under the heading 'free skools'. The term encompasses both activities that take place in the somewhat *ad hoc* surroundings of a cafe or a member's home, as well as more traditionally educational 'school' settings. An important example of the latter is the Sudbury school: a form of schooling that started in Massachusetts and has spread throughout America and Europe. In these schools, learners are free to design their own programme of study on a day-to-day basis. As with other forms of learning in this section, Sudbury schools value voluntary participation, learning from one another and democratic community.

Alternative types of schooling: Steiner and Montessori

The two most widespread and rapidly expanding alternative school approaches have developed from the educational philosophies of Rudolph Steiner and Maria Montessori. Both advocated education systems that offered a different form of culture of learning in the classroom. In continental Europe, Montessori and Steiner's Waldorf schools have both been integrated into the state system.

There are many similarities in the cultures of learning the two types of schools cultivate. Both conceive of learning as a 'whole child' experience – intellectual or academic advancement is not distinguished from or prioritised over psychological, spiritual, physical and mental development. In fact, the starting point of both educational philosophies is a deep respect for the child as a creative and spiritual individual. Neither base learning on the acquisition of knowledge via text books, preferring to enable children to learn at their own unique pace. Both stress the importance of nature and the natural environment, believing children need to be protected from the pressures and artifice of modern society (especially technology) if they are to develop positively.

Both schools offer an alternative to the year group characteristic of mainstream formal schooling. Steiner–Waldorf school children are in groups with other children of the same age, but they would tend to have one teacher throughout their schooling (or at least until the age of 14 when more 'academic' disciplines are introduced into the curriculum). This allows for deep and personal relationships to be fostered between learner and teacher (Woods *et al.*, 2005). Montessori schools typically divide children into groups with an age range of three years. Teachers work individually with each child, directed by the needs and interests of each individual. In fact, in comparison with formal schooling, the teacher often does very little. The teacher carefully observes the children, who are encouraged to be active and autonomous learners. Within these groups, older children teach younger children (Lillard, 2005). As a result, while the Steiner–Waldorf school day is very ordered (though very differently from mainstream schooling), Montessori schools appear relatively unstructured.

One of the main differences between these two alternatives is their relationship with the everyday world. Montessori schools introduce children to practical skills very early on. They are taught about the culture of the world they live in and are given access to everyday objects to play with. Through 'play-work', they learn how to pack a suitcase or how to knit. In contrast, Steiner–Waldorf schools can appear rather otherworldly. A central facet of the school day is *eurhythmy* – rhythmic movements designed to aid focus and concentration. Children tend to play with simple wooden toys: plastics, calculators and computers are avoided until children are around 14 years old. A great emphasis is placed on fantasy and imagination, with children encouraged to express themselves spiritually and artistically.

Critical Thinking Task

At this stage of the chapter, you have encountered a range of alternative cultures of learning. It is now time to recap and to use this material. Reread the sections on the following (you might want to research these topics more widely):

- AS Neill;
- Paulo Freire;
- Unschooling;
- Free skools;
- Steiner–Waldorf;
- Montessori.

In a small group, consider the following questions:

- what cultures of learning do these six alternatives have in common? (distinguish between values and practices);
- how do they differ?;
- what characteristics are shared with formal schooling?;
- where are the most evident differences? (be careful not to oversimplify/distort 'all formal schooling');

- by studying alternative visions and practices of learning and culture, what can you learn about formal schooling?

Now find out about another alternative to formal schooling – you might look at Forest or Reggio Emilia schools for instance. To what extent does your new alternative correspond with/contradict your previous responses?

Finally, divide into two groups. In these groups organise a debate on the motion:

Children are better off learning outside formal education where they can have more control over their own learning.

Alternative cultures of learning and lessons for schooling

As you have been reading this chapter, you might have been thinking that many of these ideas and strategies have become dimensions of formal schooling. It is certainly true that educational policy makers appear open to alternative conceptualisations of learning. An emphasis on pupil and parental choice is driving forwards a culture of innovation in learning. For instance, the ideas and practices of Steiner and Montessori schooling are increasingly evident in British state schooling. Hereford Steiner Academy became the first state-funded Steiner school in 2008 and UK state-funded Montessori primary schools have been in existence since 2005.

So it is not the case that a sharp distinction exists between formal schooling (with one culture of learning) and a range of alternative learning sites (that offer entirely different cultures). (*NB always be suspicious of any claim that all formal schooling consists of . . .*) Nevertheless, formal schooling might offer more enriching and stimulating learning opportunities if teachers and policy makers take further lessons from alternatives like those outlined during this chapter provide. In particular, alternatives tend to place greater emphasis on:

- play and enjoyment;
- voluntary and self-directed learning;
- relevance;
- community;
- educating the 'whole child';
- personal relationships and the importance of self-esteem.

Critical Thinking Task

Progressive learning strategies are increasingly evident around the fringes of formal state education. These innovative mainstream approaches to learning are generally targeted at less 'traditional' learners (adults, children from deprived communities, disaffected learners). Have a look at these current initiatives:

- taking learning outside formal school environments – *Playing for Success* and *Study Support Centres;*
- learning is for everyone – *lifelong learning;*

- online learning communities – Notschool.net (**www.literacytrust.org.uk/socialinclusion/ youngpeople/notschoolpractice.html**)
- connecting education with the rest of life – SureStart.

In your small group, discuss the following.

- Why might policy makers develop innovative initiatives for non-traditional learners?
- What types of learning experiences might these non-traditional learners need/be looking for/be afraid of?
- Do you think these initiatives are attempting to stimulate a culture of learning? How?

Two areas where formal education does seem to be taking lessons from informal education are in e-learning and in fostering connections between schooling and community. These are considered and illustrated in turn.

Community education

A link between ideas of community and of education is nothing new. All activities that take place within a community with broadly educational intent fall under this heading. As you can see then, the idea of 'community education' broadens the scope, range of activities, definitions and purposes of learning. Sessions might be run by charities, voluntary groups, businesses or interest groups. The term implies a wide range of activities and settings, including:

- theatre/drama/music groups;
- mother and toddler groups;
- youth organisations;
- legal, citizens advice;
- cafes, leisure centres;
- internet sites;
- museums and galleries;
- accredited lifelong learning courses;
- outdoor centres.

In recent years the 'formal' and 'informal' have increasingly overlapped – with connections encouraged between the 'community' and formal education, and with the 'formal education' quality assurance processes increasingly applied to informal settings. This is largely due to a change in emphasis from the individual in the 1980s to the community in the early twenty-first century. Since coming to power in 1997, the Labour government pursued a broadly 'communitarian' agenda. From this perspective, strong communities are viewed as healthy environments, able to foster both social regeneration and social inclusion. Grass-roots community activities are seen as a key way of tackling social problems and improving inner cities. A number of policies devised around the millennium focused on community development. These included:

- SureStart;
- education action zones;
- citizenship curriculum;
- Neighbourhood Renewal Unit.

As these examples illustrate, policy makers tend to place education at the centre of community building. The intention is that educational institutions become a resource for the community and vice versa. Moreover, by making associations with the wider community, schools cease to be regarded as the sole provider of legitimate learning experiences. To continue Leadbeater's earlier comment:

Schools and universities should become more like hubs of learning, within the community, capable of extending into the community . . . More learning needs to be done at home, in offices and kitchens, in the contexts where knowledge is deployed to solve problems and add value to people's lives.

Leadbeater, 2000, page 227

There are evidently many benefits to making links between education and community:

- the potential for 'transformative learning' – to offer learning opportunities for those who have been socially excluded;
- reaching a wider audience – including traditionally 'hard to reach' and non-school age people;
- making school work relevant, purposeful and connected to the real-life experiences of learners;
- making use of the skills and expertise of members of the community;
- providing a focal point (a physical space) for the community to meet and collaborate with each other;
- helping to foster a positive community spirit of togetherness, trust, respect, confidence and pride.

Practical Task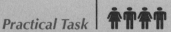

One of the more interesting current attempts to make connections between education and community is to offer community groups the opportunity to take control of their local school. This is a strategy that has been adopted in Scandinavia. In a small group, select one from the list below:

- an Islamic community who feel mainstream schooling is ignorant to their cultural and religious needs and offers an education that is overly permissive;
- a group of men who are worried that mainstream schooling has become 'feminised' and that boys are disadvantaged;
- a group of wealthy hippies who think schooling is too aggressive, competitive and constraining for their children;
- a local community in a highly deprived area whose failing school has been closed down and they have decided to develop their own alternative rather than have their children travel to the nearest mainstream school.

Now develop the following:

- the school 'mission statement';
- the 'school ethos' – the culture of learning you would hope to foster;
- strategies you will use to engage with the community;
- a marketing document to promote your school to prospective parents/pupils.

Compare your responses with those of another group. Consider the types of circumstances where these community schools might work best and identify some of the limitations and dangers of this approach to education.

An example: 'urban village schools' and a school community?

Evidence from the USA has suggested that an important way of improving children's educational performance (particularly in inner cities) is by reducing the size of the school. A large school is simply too large to enable community sentiment to develop. The sense of anonymity and insecurity a child feels when leaving a 'cosy' primary school and moves to a large secondary school is viewed by some as a key component in educational under-achievement. In recent years, the movement to have 'urban village schools' has gained force and the debate has spread to Europe. As part of the 'Building Schools for the Future' initiative in the UK, some vast comprehensives are being rebuilt as a series of smaller schools. In effect, this creates five or six semi-autonomous 'schools within schools', as illustrated in Figure 8.1:

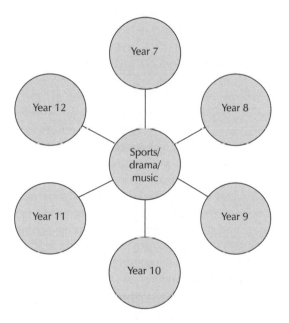

Figure 8.1
Schools within schools

The main proponent of these ideas in the UK is Dr James Wetz, who has argued that consistent contact with the same teachers and peers, alongside a more nurturing whole-school culture, supports learners who would otherwise become disaffected (Wetz, 2008). Others are less convinced. A systematic review of the literature recently found little consistency in the evidence (Evidence for Policy and Practice Information and Co-ordinating Centre (EPPI), 2004). While some pupils seem to perform better in smaller schools, others seem to prefer larger schools. There is no clear optimum size for a school it would seem.

Learning online – a new e-learning culture?

The advancement of a 'digital age' has had a tremendous impact on education, as well as on the links between education and community. The increasing range of 'new communities' (promoted through, and existing in, cyberspace) and new ways of accessing communities open up all sorts of emergent learning opportunities. Children and young people are 'digital natives', having grown up and been immersed in the 'digital revolution'. This gives them genuine potential to participate in and take ownership of their own learning. Through his influential series of 'hole-in-the-wall' experiments in India, Mitra (2006) has demonstrated the potential of computers and the internet as *self-organising systems*, where children can learn for themselves with minimal intervention.

Extensive investment and research into ICT and e-learning is taking place and government agencies like BECTA (British Educational Communications and Technology Agency) are leading the way in the innovative use of technology in schools and colleges. Clearly, electronic and mobile technology has enormous potential to reshape learning and teaching. An innovative culture of e-learning might include the use of:

- the *internet* to democratise the learning experience through active discovery;
- enhanced *web 2.0* technology to develop more creative and collaborative online learning space, such as *bookmarking* which enables students to take ownership in organising and sharing academic materials;
- *wikis* to develop collaborative resources or group assessments;
- *VLEs* (virtual learning environments) to reinforce group identity through tools such as discussion boards;
- *virtual reality* facilities such as *notschool.net* and *Second Life* as a way of providing more creative and expansive learning environments and alternatives to face-to-face classroom encounters;
- *blogs* to enable learners to create their own personal learning environments;
- *podcasting* as a way of giving learners wider access to learning materials;
- *electronic resources* (e-journals, e-newspapers) to make learning material more accessible;
- *interactive whiteboards* to bring wider and more engaging material into the classroom;
- *mobile phones* to facilitate communication between learners;
- student-produced *video* extracts to give learners greater ownership of their learning;
- sites like *YouTube* as a way of making learning connected to real-life experiences;
- *social networking sites* to enable students to cultivate learning communities;
- *wireless technology* to enable learning to take place anywhere;
- a range of *technologies* to open up opportunities to learners with special educational needs – for instance, using ipods to record lectures.

Of course, there are also many dangers associated with the rapidly expanding use of ICT to promote learning. It may be that such technology creates a new learning culture of digital 'haves' and 'have-nots'. For example, older learners might not have the skills and experience of younger 'digital natives'. More-wealthy parents can afford the newer, more effective equipment. All-singing e-lessons might give the impression of an innovative culture of learning but may be, in reality, reinforced and repackaged 'chalk and talk' pedagogy. Certain aspects of digitisation might be 'social' but others are likely to be 'anti-social': many aspects of digital technology result in a lack of human interaction, while others lead to new dangers such as e-grooming and access to inappropriate websites – see Carr-Chellman (2005) for a comprehensive critique.

Educational practitioners must think carefully about why, how and what e-learning opportunities they promote. They must ask questions like: 'Who has access?'; 'How structured are learning experiences?'; 'How far can tasks be supervised?'; 'Does providing access to e-material equate to knowledge and understanding?'; and 'How safe is this?'.

Critical Thinking Task

The relationship between learning and technology has been the focus of much discussion in recent years. As you have seen, digitisation impacts on a wide variety of educational practices and experiences. There are clear benefits associated with technological developments, but many educationalists have raised concerns about potential harmful effects. Consider the new possibilities and the threats that advances in technology provide for learning.

Use the following websites to help with these tasks:

- Bringing Educational Creativity to All (**www.becta.org.uk**)
- Naace (**www.naace.co.uk**)
- Futurelab (**www.futurelab.org.uk**)
- The Innovative Teachers Network (**www.innovativeteachers.com**)
- InterActive Education (**www.interactiveeducation.ac.uk**)

- Identify five diverse examples of the current use of technology in education – not just for educational resources! (e.g. the use of text messaging to monitor attendance).
- What does current research tell us about ICT and education?
- What 'twenty first century skills' will education need to cultivate? Provide some evidence.
- What opportunities are there to reduce educational inequalities (class, gender, ethnicity, age, region) through the use of ICT in the classroom? Provide some evidence.
- What opportunities are there for pupils with learning difficulties? Look out for the term 'e-inclusion'.
- What do you think about the growing number of sites where teachers can share/gather e-learning lesson plans/innovative ideas?
- Select an example of an e-learning task – what are the benefits and limitations of this approach?
- What do you see as the main dangers with an increase in the use of technology in education?
- How are you most likely to use ICT in your first few years of teaching or in education-related employment?

An example: 'Enquiring Minds' – e-learning and an alternative curriculum in schools

Enquiring Minds was a three-year research pilot developed by Futurelab and aimed at *preparing children for a future characterised by rapid social, technological and cultural change* (Enquiring Minds, 2008). Running from 2005 to 2008, it was piloted with Key Stage 3 pupils, offering an alternative curriculum at two Bristol schools and has since been adopted by a growing number of schools. The project, which aimed to develop opportunities for pupils to learn independently and create their own knowledge, was based on a vision:

. . . for how school might be if more responsibility for deciding on the content of lessons was given to students . . . we propose a vision for meaningful learning that starts from a principle of making visible and valuing students' own ideas, interests and concerns, and for meaningful teaching which expands and extends from there.

Enquiring Minds, 2008

Making use of digital technologies, pupils selected and then conducted their own research over an extended period of time. The purpose was to identify strategies flexible enough to enable learners to learn in their own way and at their own pace, within the confines of the national curriculum and existing school structures. It is difficult to envisage how pupil–teacher co-designed curriculum can co-exist with testing systems and prescribed curriculum. The two seem fundamentally incompatible. Nevertheless, Enquiring Minds signals a significant cultural shift in our understanding of effective learning.

On its own, this might seem like a rather small initiative, but Enquiring Minds is indicative of a rapid expansion in e-learning educational initiatives targeted at mainstream schooling over recent years (from charities, foundations, university researchers, businesses). Greater local autonomy in schools has allowed for small-scale innovations to be implemented. Another example is the Royal Society for the encouragement of Arts, Manufactures and Commerce (RSA) 'Opening Minds' project, which has developed an alternative 'competence-led' curriculum that is now in use in some schools (RSA, 1999). Likewise, the Future Schools Network (FSN) consists of 50 schools in the UK who are working together to develop innovative schooling for the twenty-first century and to engage with educational policy makers. (FSN, 2008).

Practical Task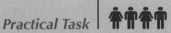

During this chapter, you have encountered a range of alternative cultures of learning. Now think about what these alternative curricula/lessons might look like in practice. By designing medium-term and lesson plans, you can reflect on how teachers and learners might experience these alternatives in their daily working lives.

Conduct some research into the details of Enquiring Minds and Opening Minds initiatives. There are plenty of resources and learning material accessible through both websites. You might also find a video on the website Teachers TV (**www.teachers.tv**) useful. This shows the Enquiring Minds project in action in a school in Bristol.

Now divide into small groups and undertake the following tasks.

- Design a series of connected lessons that make use of these strategies.
- Develop a short role-play of part of a session and deliver it to the rest of your group.
- Now ask your audience how they would feel as students undertaking such a session within existing educational structures.
- What do you see as the benefits and limitations of these types of learning and teaching practices?
- How might they impact on a culture of learning in the school?
- Do you think such strategies can run alongside the national curriculum and existing assessment structures?
- At what stages of education might such strategies be most effective? Why?

What could learning be in contemporary culture?

To start to conceive of a radically different form of learning it is worth returning to the time when progressive educational ideas were at their height. In 1973, Ivan Illich wrote *Deschooling society*. Earlier in the chapter you have encountered his critique of the institutionalised and professionalised version of learning promoted through formal schooling. In Chapter 6 of this short but influential book, Illich offers an alternative culture of learning based on the notion of *learning webs* (Illich, 1973, pages 72–104).

He argued that education should be based on informality rather than formality and be widespread and not limited to particular age groups, times and buildings, and that participation should be self-determined rather than compulsory. Illich envisaged an education 'system' where anyone would have access to resources to learn at any age. Provision would be established to enable those who wanted to share knowledge to contact people who wanted to learn from them. This included four dimensions:

- *reference services to educational objects*: a way of identifying and making contact with places where one can learn (museums, libraries, laboratories, theatres . . .) – learning can take place in all sorts of settings, not just schools;
- *skill exchanges*: a space for people to advertise the skills they possess and would be happy to teach, and what they would want in return (this could be financial or an alternative skill) – it is not just teachers who possess skills they can pass on;
- *peer matching*: a space where people can advertise the things they want to learn, so that they are able to form learning groups – voluntary groups of shared-interest learners are better than groups that are arbitrarily enforced to be together;
- *reference services to educators at large*: a directory of 'educators' with testimonials from former learners – a list of comments by past learners to estimate the merits of a teacher, rather than a teaching qualification.

This all might sound rather utopian and unrealistic. But the more you look at these four dimensions, the more attractive they might appear. Certainly, you use most of these strategies when conducting other parts of your life. You will have vivid learning memories from visits to museums or theatres. You will have looked in the yellow pages or in the local paper to find a plumber or electrician. You might belong to a networking organisation or a sports/hobbies team. You will have chosen services based on recommendations. Or if you use internet sites like ebay, you will have evaluated a listing by referring to the amount of positive feedback the seller has received. So if these strategies are good enough for the rest of your life, why not for your education?

Furthermore, increasing interest in, and use of, ICT and community in formal education seems to provide the ideal grounds for revisiting Illich's conception. The numbers of people over the compulsory schooling age accessing learning opportunities is growing. Changes in the nature of society and work mean such trends are likely to continue. These learners seek informality, voluntary participation and community learning networks (or 'webs'). The internet is already used as a source of social networking and skills sharing. As technology develops, the need for a specific physical educational space reduces. Alongside this, the opportunities for people with shared interests and learning needs increases. Unlimited by physical constraints, new 'virtual' communities can come in and out of existence very quickly. Fluid learning spaces can enable people to have temporary membership of these communities. These new cultures of learning are in their infancy, but they are growing speedily.

Nevertheless, it is difficult to see an educational culture consisting of voluntary and informal learning networks supersede the formal structures that have developed over the twentieth century. This might not offer a viable alternative. But it does seem plausible that the latter might shrink as the potential for the former increases. There will always be a place for 'formal' early socialisation and for the acquisition of basic skills such as numeracy and literacy. But the learners of today have the potential to take greater ownership of, and responsibility for, their learning experiences. The population is increasingly fragmented, complex and pluralised, with the skills and confidence to access information, materials and services. In contemporary culture, is it feasible to conceive of formal, compulsory schooling ending at 11 or 12? Could it possibly be replaced with an extensive network of community and e-learning opportunities open to everybody, whoever or wherever they are?

Chapter Summary

After reading this chapter, you should recognise that:

- There is substantial criticism of a formal schooling system as overly professionalised and tightly controlled and monitored. This can result in a culture that equates learning with assessment success. It also restricts learning to the narrow confines of specific age groups and institutions.
- Informal cultures of learning provide opportunities for people of all ages to make autonomous choices about their own learning and can help to include and empower them. Alternatives place emphasis on the learner as a self-directed social actor.
- Formal and informal educations borrow values and strategies from one another. They are not two entirely distinct entities. Formal education might be dominated by assessment and audit regimes, but informal learning opportunities are increasingly incorporated. This is most evident in community and e-learning provision.
- The characteristics of contemporary culture 'fit' with the loose, voluntary, diverse and fluid nature of informal educational arrangements.

Research focus

Background

One of the most common criticisms of formal school in recent years is that a preoccupation with assessment and audit has a limiting effect on a culture of learning. At the same time, formal education, and the learning opportunities that it provides, is frequently viewed as the means by which young people can become engaged and empowered. These features are evident in the following two articles:

- Miles, S (2007) Feeing 10 feet tall: creative inclusion in a community of practice. *British Journal of Sociology of Education*, 28 (4): 505–18.
- James, D and Diment, K (2003) Going Underground? Learning and assessment in an ambiguous space. *Journal of Vocational Education and Training*, 55 (4): 407–22.

In reading these two articles, consider the qualities of the learning sites and the learners and teachers. What do the positive learning experiences and outcomes depend on? How far are they sustainable?

Schools and community

Progressive and radical educationalists see the capacity of education as a community-building process and as a means of liberating people. Many writers have focused on the power of education to enfranchise and liberate people who are at the margins of society or who live in deprived urban areas.

Read the chapter entitled 'Education and Conscientizao' (37–52) in Freire and Part 3 (127–201) of Anyon's book:

- Freire, P (2005) *Education for critical consciousness*. London: Continuum International.
- Anyon, J (2005) *Radical possibilities: public policy, urban education, and a new social movement*. Abingdon: Routledge.

In these chapters, you will see a range of strategies and examples for fostering a 'culture of democracy' through education and community links. Both argue that, through education, people can learn to see their social position, can develop the skills and tools to mobilise and can transform their community for themselves. Critically evaluate the localised grass-roots educational community projects, as outlined by Anyon. How far do agree that education is (or should be) a catalyst for social change?

Progressive perspectives and practices

The following articles consider the position of progressivism in education today. Stronach reassesses Neill's educational philosophy that you encountered earlier in the chapter. You also read about Enquiring Minds, a pilot project that makes use of ICT and community to provide engaging and self-directed learning experiences.

- Stronach, I and Piper H (2008) Can liberal education make a comeback? The case of 'relational touch' at Summerhill School. *American Educational Research Journal*, 45 (1): 6–37.
- Morgan, J and Williamson, B (2008) *Enquiring Minds: schools, knowledge and educational change*. Bristol: Futurelab. **www.enquiringminds.org.uk/our_research/reports_and_papers/year3_report/**

Read these two articles carefully. Remember the first is based on a small private 'progressive' school, whereas the second outlines and justifies a 'progressive' intervention in a state secondary school. Identify the values and strategies explored during the papers. With reference to your reading throughout the book, assess these accounts of learning in contemporary culture.

References

Acton, A (1989) Democratic practice in a primary school, in Harber, C and Meighan, R (eds) *The democratic school: educational management and the practice of democracy*. Ticknall: Education Now.

Ajegbo, K (2007) *Curriculum review: diversity and citizenship*. London: DfES.

Andersen, ML and Taylor, HF (2005) *Sociology: understanding a diverse society*. New York: Thompson Wadsworth.

Anderson, B (1983) *Imagined communities: reflections on the origin and spread of nationalism*. London: Verso.

Anyon, J (2005) *Radical possibilities: public policy, urban education, and a new social movement*. Abingdon: Routledge.

Apple, M (2004) *Ideology and curriculum*, 3rd edition. London: Routledge.

Archer, L (2003) *Race, masculinity and schooling*. Buckingham: Open University Press.

Archer, L and Francis, B (2006) *Understanding minority ethnic achievement: race, gender, class and 'success'*. London: Routledge.

Archer, L and Yamashita, H (2003) 'Knowing their limits'? Identities, inequalities and inner city school leavers' post-16 aspirations'. *Journal of Education Policy*, 18 (1): 53–9.

Aries, P (1996) *Centuries of childhood*. London: Pimlico.

Atkins, L (2008) Travelling hopefully: an exploration of the limited possibilities for Level 1 students in the English further education system. *Research in Post-Compulsory Education*, 13(2): 195–204.

Bache, I (2003) Governing though governance: education policy under New Labour. *Political Studies*, 51(2) pp 300–314.

Ball, S (2008) *The education debate: policy and politics in the twenty-first century*. Bristol: Policy Press.

Ball, S (1981) *Beachside comprehensive*. Cambridge: Cambridge University Press.

Barber, M (1997) *The learning game: arguments for an education revolution*. London: Indigo.

Baudrillard, J (2004) *The Gulf War did not take place* (Paul Patton translator). Sydney: Power Publications.

Bauman, A and May, T (2001) *Thinking sociologically*, 2nd edition. Oxford: Blackwell.

Baumann, G (2006) Introduction: nation-state, schools and civil enculturation, in Schiffauer, W, Baumann, G, Kastoryano, R and Vertovec, S (eds) *Civil enculturation: nation-state, schools and ethnic difference in the Netherlands, Britain, Germany and France*. New York: Berghan Books.

Bauman, Z (1997) *Postmodernity and its discontents*. Cambridge: Polity Press.

Bauman, Z (2000) *Liquid modernity*. Cambridge: Polity Press.

Bauman, Z (2001) *The individualized society*. Cambridge: Polity Press.

Beck, C (1993) Postmodernism, pedagogy, and philosophy of education. *Philosophy of Education*, **www.ed.uiuc.edu/eps/PES-Yearbook/93_docs/BECK.HTM** (accessed 19 February 2009).

Beck, V, Fuller, A and Unwin, L (2006) 'Safety in stereotypes? The impact of gender and 'race' on young people's perceptions of their post-compulsory education and labour market opportunities' *British Educational Research Journal*, 32 (5): 667–86.

Becker, HS (1952) Social-class variations in the teacher-pupil relationship. *Journal of Educational Sociology*, 15: 451–65.

Bem, SL (1989) Genital knowledge and gender constancy in pre-school children. *Child Development*, 60: 649–62.

Bennett, A (1999) Subcultures or neo-tribes? Rethinking the relationship between youth, style and musical taste. *Sociology*, 33 (3): 599–617.

Bernstein, B (1996) *Pedagogy, symbolic control and identity theory, research, critique*. London: Taylor and Francis.

Bielaczyc, K and Collins, A (1999) *Learning communities in classrooms: advancing knowledge for a lifetime. National Association of Secondary School Principals*, 1999, 83 (4): 4–10.

Bocock, R (1992) The Cultural Formations of Modern Society, in Hall, S and Gieben, B (eds) *Formations of modernity*. Cambridge: Polity with Open University Press.

Bourdieu, P and Passeron, J (1977) *Reproduction in education, society and culture*. London: Sage.

Bowles, S and Gintis, H (1976) *Schooling in capitalist America*. London: Routledge.

Bruner, J (1997) *The culture of education*. Cambridge, MA: Harvard University Press.

Buzzelli, C and Johnston, B (2002) *The moral dimensions of teaching: language, power and culture in classroom interactions*. Abingdon: Routledge/Falmer Press.

Campaign for Learning (2008) **www.campaign-for-learning.org.uk/cfl/index.asp** (accessed 23 February 2009).

Carr-Chellman, A (2005) *Global perspectives on e-learning: rhetoric and reality*. London: Sage.

Centre for Contemporary Cultural Studies (CCCS) (1982) *The empire strikes back*. London: Hutchinson.

Chapman, K (1986) *The sociology of schools*. London: Routledge.

Citizenship Education Review Group (2005) *A systematic review of the impact of citizenship education on student learning and achievement*. London: Institute of Education.

Civitas (2007) School curriculum corrupted by politics, **www.civitas.org.uk/press/prcs Corruption.php** (accessed 23 February 2009).

Clarke, J (2003) Managing and delivering welfare, in Alcock, P, Erskine, A and May, M (eds) *The students' companion to social policy*. Oxford: Blackwell.

Claxton, G (1999) *Wise up: how to live the learning life*. London: Continuum.

Claxton, G (2000) Integrity and uncertainty – why young people need doubtful teachers, in Best, R, Lodge, C and Watkins, C (2000) *Tomorrow's schools: towards integrity*. London: Routledge.

Claxton, G (2002) *Building learning power*. Bristol: TLO.

Claxton, G (2004) *Learning to learn: a key goal in a 21st century curriculum*. London: Qualifications and Curriculum Authority. **www.qca.org.uk/libraryAssets/media/11469_ claxton_learning_to_learn.pdf** (accessed 3 March 2009).

Claxton, G (2006) *Expanding the capacity to learn: a new end for education?* Keynote address at British Educational Research Association Annual Conference, September 2006, Warwick University.

Coffield, F, Moseley, D, Hall, E and Ecclestone, K (2004) *Should we be using learning styles? What research has to say to practice*. Learning and Skills Research Centre, Trowbridge: Cromwell Press.

Cohen, E (2002) Classroom processes, in Levinson, PW, Cookson, AR and Sadovnik, AR (eds) *Education and sociology: an encyclopedia*. New York: Routledge Falmer.

Cohen, S (1997) Symbols of trouble, in Gelder, K and Thornton, S (eds) *The subcultures reader*. London: Routledge.

Coles, R (1997) *The moral intelligence of children*. London: Bloomsbury.

Collins, A and Bielaczyc, K (1999) The enculturation of educational thinking. *Journal of the Learning Sciences*, 8 (1): 129–38.

Commonwealth Immigration Advisory Council (1964) *Second report*. London: HMSO.

Connolly, P (2004) *Boys and schooling in the early years*. London: Routledge.

Connolly, P (2006) Summary statistics, educational achievement gaps and the ecological fallacy. *Oxford Review of Education*, 32 (2): 235–52.

Cooper, B (1998) Using Bernstein and Bourdieu to understand children's difficulties with 'realistic' mathematics testing: an exploratory study. *Qualitative Studies in Education*, 11 (4): 511–32.

Corrigan, P (1979) *Schooling the Smash Street kids*. London: Macmillan.

Coulby, D (2000) *Beyond the national curriculum: curricular centralism and cultural diversity in Europe and the USA*. London: Falmer.

Cunningham, L and Reich, J (2005) *Culture and values: a survey of the humanities*. Belmont: Wadsworth Publishers.

Curtis, R and Wilcock, H (2003) *Developing teaching and learning*. Solihull: Inspection and Advisory Service.

Curtis, W (2006) *A-level learning cultures in further education: an ethnographic study of teaching and learning*. PhD Thesis, University of the West of England, Bristol.

Curtis, W (2008) Learning identities and characters of studentship: an alternative to learning styles. *Educational Futures*, 1 (2): 29–41.

David, M (2003) Education, in Alcock, P, Erskine, A and May, M (eds) *The students' companion to social policy*. Oxford: Blackwell.

Demos (2004) *About learning: report of the Learning Working Group*. London: Demos.

Department for Education and Employment (DfEE) (1998) *The learning age: A renaissance for a new Britain*. London: DfEE.

Department for Education and Science (DES) (1963) *English for immigrants*. London: DES.

Descartes, R (2008) *Meditations of first philosophy: with selections from the objections and replies* (Oxford World Classics). Oxford: Oxford University Press.

Dewey, J (1997) *Democracy and education: an introduction to the philosophy of education*. New York: The Free Press.

Diamond, J (1997) *Guns, germs and steel: a short history of everybody for the last 13 000 years*. New York: Norton.

Dupré, L (2004) *The enlightenment and the intellectual foundations of modern culture*. London: Yale University Press.

Durkheim, E (2003) *Moral education: a study in the theory and application of the sociology of education*. New York: Dover Publications.

Eagleton, T (2000) *The Idea of culture* Oxford: Blackwell Publishing.

Elias, N, Dunning, E, Goudsblom, J, Jephcott, E, Mennell, S (2000) *The civilizing process: sociogenetic and psychogenetic investigations*, revised edition. Oxford: Blackwell Publishing.

Elias, MJ, Zins, JE, Weissberg, RP, Frey et al. (1997) *Promoting social and emotional learning: guidelines for educators* Alexandria, VA: Association for Supervision and Curriculum Development.

Enquiring Minds (2008) **www.enquiringminds.org.uk/what_is_enquiring_minds/** (accessed 3 March 2009).

Evidence for Policy and Practice Information and Co-ordinating Centre (EPPI) (2004) *Secondary school size: a systematic review*. London: Social Science Research Unit, Institute of Education.

Evers, C (2006) Culture, cognitive pluralism and rationality. *Educational Philosophy and Theory*, 39 (4): 364–82.

Fielding, M (2001) Beyond the rhetoric of student voice: new departures or new constraints in the transformation of 21st century schooling? *Forum*, 43 (2): 100–110.

Fielding, M (2007) Beyond 'voice': new roles, relations, and contexts in researching with young people. *Discourse: Studies in the Cultural Politics of Education*, 28 (3): 301–10.

Fischer, SR (2004) *A history of writing*. London: Reaktion Books.

Foucault, M (1991) *Discipline and punish. The birth of the prison*. Harmondsworth: Penguin Books.

France, A (2007) *Understanding youth in late modernity*. Maidenhead: Open University Press with McGraw Hill.

Francis, B (2000) The gender subject: students' subject preferences and discussions of gender and subject ability. *Oxford Review of Education*, 26 (1): 35–48.

Franklin, B (2004) Education, education and indoctrination! Packaging politics and the three 'Rs', *Journal of Education Policy*, 19 (3): 255–70.

Franklin, S (2006) VAKing out learning styles – why the notion of 'learning styles' is unhelpful to teachers. *Education*, 3 (13): 81–7.

Freire, P (2005) *Education for critical consciousness*. London: Continuum International

Freire, P and Macedo, D (2000) *Pedagogy of the oppressed: 30th anniversary edition*. London: Continuum International.

Frosh, S, Phoenix, A and Pattman, R (2002) *Young masculinities: understanding boys in contemporary society*. Basingstoke: Palgrave.

Future Schools Network (2008) **www.thersa.org/projects/education/future-schools-network** (accessed 23 February 2009).

Gaine, C and George, R (1999) *Gender, 'race' and class in schooling*, 2nd edition. London: Routledge Falmer.

Gardner, H (1999) *Intelligence reframed: multiple intelligences for the 21st century*. New York: Basic Books.

Gatto, J (2002) *Dumbing us down: the hidden curriculum of compulsory schooling*, 2nd edition. Gabriola Island: New Society Publishers.

Gellner, E (1996) The coming of nationalism and its interpretation: the myths of nation and class, in Balakrishnan, G and Anderson, B (eds) *Mapping the nation*. London: Verso.

Gewirtz, S, Dickson, M and Power, S (2004) Unravelling a 'spun' policy: a case study of the constitutive role of 'spin' in the education policy process' *Journal of Education Policy*, 19 (3): 321–42.

Giddens, A (1991) *Modernity and self-identity: self and society in the late modern age*. Cambridge: Polity Press.

Giddens, A (2002) *Runaway world*. London: Profile Books Limited.

Gillborn, D (1995) *Racism and antiracism in real schools: theory, policy, practice*. Buckingham: Open University Press.

Gillborn, D and Mirza, HS (2000) *Educational inequality: mapping race, class and gender*. London: OFSTED.

Gillborn, D and Youdell, D (1999) *Rationing education: policy, practice, reform and equity*. Buckingham: Open University Press.

Ginott, H (1972) *Teacher and child: a book for parents and teachers*. New York: MacMillan.

Giroux, H (1988) *Teachers as intellectuals: towards a critical pedagogy of learning*. Westport: Greenwood Publishing.

Giroux, H (1989) *Schooling for democracy: critical pedagogy in the modern age*. New York: Routledge.

Giroux, H (1997) Race, pedagogy, and whiteness in *Dangerous Minds*. *Cineaste*, 22 (4): 46–49.

Giroux, H (2004) *The terror of neoliberalism: authoritarianism and the eclipse of democracy*. Boulder: Paradigm.

Glatter, R (1999) From struggling to juggling: towards a redefinition of the field of educational management. *Educational Management and Administration*, 27 (3): 253–66.

Goldenberg, C (1991). *Instructional conversations and their classroom application*. Berkeley: National Centre for Research on Cultural Diversity and Second Language Learning.

Goleman, D (1996) *Emotional intelligence: why it can matter more than IQ*. London: Bloomsbury Publishing.

Goodhart, D (2004) The discomfort of strangers *The Guardian* [online] 24 February. **www.guardian.co.uk/race/story/0,11374,1154684,00.html** (accessed 3 March 2009)

Goodlad, S and Hirst, B (1989) *Peer tutoring: a guide to learning by teaching.* New York: Nicols Publishing.

Gove, J and Watt, S (2000) Identity and gender, in Woodward H (ed) *Questioning identity: gender, class, nation.* London: Routledge.

Grenfell, M (2004) Bourdieu in the classroom, in Olssen, M (ed) *Culture and learning: access and opportunity in the classroom.* Greenwich: Information Age, pages 49–72.

Habermas, J (1981) *The theory of communicative action.* London: Beacon Press.

Hague, R and Harrop, M (2004) *Comparative government and politics: an introduction.* Basingstoke: Palgrave MacMillan.

Hall, K (1995) 'There's a time to act English and a time to act Indian': the politics of identity among British-Sikh teenagers, in Stephens, S (ed) *Children and the politics of culture.* Chichester: Princeton University Press.

Hall, S and Jefferson, T (ed) (1995) *Resistance through rituals: youth subcultures in post-war Britain.* London: Routledge.

Hamilton, P (1996) The enlightenment and the birth of social science, in Hall, S, Held, D, Hubert, D and Thompson, K (eds) *Modernity: an introduction to modern societies.* Oxford: Blackwell.

Hargreaves, D (1976) Reactions to labelling, Hammersley, M and Woods, P (eds) *The process of schooling.* London: Routledge.

Hartley, D (1997) *Re-schooling society.* London: Falmer Press.

Harvey, D (1989) *The condition of postmodernity: an enquiry into the origins of cultural change.* Oxford: Blackwell.

Haste, H and Abrahams, S. (2008) Morality, *culture* and the dialogic self: taking cultural pluralism seriously. *Journal of Moral Education*, 37 (3): 377–94.

Haydon, G (2006) Respect for persons and for cultures as a basis for national and global citizenship. *Journal of Moral Education*, 35 (4): 457–71.

Hearn, J (2006) *Rethinking nationalism: a critical introduction.* Basingstoke: Palgrave Macmillan.

Hickman, L and Alexander, T (1998) *The essential Dewey volume 1: pragmatism, education, democracy.* Bloomington: Indiana University Press.

Hinsliff, G (2005) Schools blasted for Yo! Sushi take on history: lessons put too much focus on the effects of war in shaping Britain's identity, claim experts. *The Observer* 18 December.

Holt, J (1990) *How children fail.* Harmondsworth: Penguin Books.

Holt, J (1997) *Growing without schooling: a record of a grassroots movement: 001.* Wakefield, MA: Holt Associates.

Howard, M (2005) Comment and analysis: talk about the British dream: integration is about the values we share, not traditions that divide us. *The Guardian* 17 August.

Hutchings, B (2006) *Principles of enquiry-based learning.* Manchester: Centre for Excellence in Enquiry-Based Learning University of Manchester.

Illich, I (1973) *Deschooling society.* Harmondsworth: Penguin Books.

Irvine, JJ and York, E (1995) Research on learning styles, in Banks, JA and Banks, CA (eds) *Handbook of research on multicultural education.* New York: Macmillan.

James, D and Bloomer, M. (2001) *Cultures and learning in further education.* BERA Annual Conference, September, 2001.

James, D and Diment, K (2003) Going underground? Learning and assessment in an ambiguous space. *Journal of Vocational Education and Training*, 55 (4): 407–22.

Johnson, B (2005) This is a turning point: we have to fly the flag for Britishness again. The *Daily Telegraph*, 14 July.

Jones, R (1999) *Teaching racism or tackling it? Multicultural stories from white beginning teachers*. Stoke on Trent: Trentham.

Karpov, Y (2006) *The neo-Vygotskian approach to child development*. Cambridge: Cambridge University Press.

Keddie, N (1971) Classroom knowledge, in Young MFD (ed) *Knowledge and control*. London: Collier Macmillan.

Kelly, A (1986) *Gender differences in teacher–pupil interaction: a meta-analytical review*. Paper presented at the British Educational Research Association Annual Conference, Bristol, September.

Kelly, AV (2004) *The curriculum: theory and practice*, 5th edition. London: Sage.

Lankshear, C, Peters, M and Knobel, M (2000) Information, knowledge and learning: some issues facing epistemology and education in a digital age. *Journal of Philosophy of Education*, 34 (1): 17–39.

Larochelle, M (2007) Disciplinary power and the school form. *Cultural Studies of Science Education*, 2 (4): 711–20.

Lawton, D (1975) *Class, culture and the curriculum*. London: Routledge.

Lawton, D and Gordon, P (2002) *A history of western educational ideas*. London: Routledge.

Leadbeater, C (2000) *Living on thin air: the new economy*. Harmondsworth: Penguin Books.

Leung, C (2001) English as an additional language: distinct curriculum focus or diffused curriculum concerns. *Language and Education*, 15 (1): 33–55.

Levinson, B and Holland, C (1996) The cultural production of the educated person: an introduction, in Levinson, B, Foley, D and Holland, C (eds) *The cultural production of the educated person: critical ethnographies of schooling and local practice*. Albany: SUNY Press.

Lillard, A (2005) *Montessori: the science behind the genius*. Oxford: Oxford University Press.

Lowe, R (ed) (1992) *Education and the second world war: studies in schooling and social change*. London: The Falmer Press.

Lyotard, J (1984) *The postmodern condition: a report on knowledge*. Manchester: Manchester University Press.

MacIntosh, M (1990) 'Caught between the two': gender and race in a Scottish school, in Patterson, F and Fewell, J (eds) *Girls in their prime: Scottish education revisited*. Edinburgh: Scottish Academic Press.

Mangan, JA (ed) (1988) *Benefits bestowed: education and British imperialism*. Manchester: Manchester University Press.

Marx, L And Mazlish, B (1996) *Progress: fact or illusion?* Ann Arbor: University of Michigan Press.

Maslow, A (1970) *Motivation and Personality*, 2nd edition. New York: Harper and Row.

Mason, M (2000) Teachers as critical mediators of knowledge. *Journal of Philosophy of Education*, 34 (2): 343–52.

Myers and Briggs Foundation (2008) **www.myersbriggs.org** (accessed 23 February 2009).

Miles, S (2007) Feeling 10 feet tall: creative inclusion in a community of practice. *British Journal of Sociology of Education*, 28 (4): 505–18.

Miller, WL, Timpson, AM and Lessnoff, MH (1996) *Political culture in contemporary britain*. Oxford: Oxford University Press.

Mirza, HS (2008) *Multiculturalism: unpacking dilemmas for teachers*. Presentation given at the Multiverse National Conference, May 2008. **www.multiverse.ac.uk/attachments/f879 98d5-c942-47af-a0e4-e0c63de2f376.doc** (accessed 23 February 2009).

Mitra, S (2006) *The hole in the wall: self-organising systems in education*. New Delhi: Tata-McGraw-Hill.

Modood, T, Berthoud, R and Nazroo, J (2002) 'Race', racism and ethnicity: a response to Ken Smith. *Sociology*, 36 (2): 419–27.

Morgan, J and Williamson, B (2008) *Enquiring Minds: schools, knowledge and educational change*. Bristol: Futurelab. **www.enquiringminds.org.uk/our_research/reports_and_papers/year3_report/** (accessed 3 March 2009).

Moyles, J (2005) (ed) *The excellence of play*, 2nd edition. Maidenhead: Open University Press.

National Curriculum Online (2008) *Statement of values*. **http://curriculum.qca.org.uk** (accessed 23 February 2009).

Nayak, A and Kehily, MJ (2008) *Gender, youth and culture: young masculinities and femininities*. Basingstoke: Palgrave Macmillan.

Not Back to School Camp (NBTSC) (2008) **www.nbtsc.org** (accessed 23 February 2009).

Neill, A (1970) *Summerhill – a radical approach to education.* Harmondsworth: Penguin Books.

Newman, E, Waller, R and Butcher, H (2008) *'Your views are important, fill in this form'. The NSS: reliable conduit for student voice or 'a useless exercise'?* Presented at British Education Studies Annual Conference, June 2008.

Nietzsche, F (1998) *Beyond good and evil: prelude to a philosophy of the future* (Oxford World Classics). Oxford: Oxford Paperbacks.

Nietzsche, F (2001) *The Gay science* (Cambridge Texts in the History of Philosophy). Williams, B (ed) Cambridge: Cambridge University Press.

Nisbet, R (1980) *History of the idea of progress*. London: Heinemann.

Osler, A (2008) Citizenship education and the Ajegbo report: re-imagining a cosmopolitan nation. *London Review of Education*, 6 (1): 11–25.

Palmer, S (2006) *Toxic childhood: how the modern world is damaging our children and what we can do about it.* London: Orion.

Parekh, B (2000) *Rethinking multiculturalism: cultural diversity and political theory.* Basingstoke: MacMillan.

Parsons, T (1964) *The social system*. New York: Free Press.

Phoenix, A (2004) Neoliberalism and masculinity: racialization and the contradictions of schooling for 11 to 14 year olds. *Youth and Society*, 36 (2): 227–46.

Postman, N and Weingartner, C (1971) *Teaching as a subversive activity*. Harmondsworth: Penguin Education.

Pring, R (2005) *Philosophy of education: aims, theory, common sense and research.* London: Continuum.

Pykett, J (2008) Making Citizens Governable? The Crick report as governmental technology. *Journal of Education Policy*, 22 (3): 301–20.

Raffo, C and Dyson, A (2007) Full service extended schools and educational inequality in urban contexts – new opportunities for progress? *Journal of Education Policy*, 22 (3): 263–82.

Ramirez, FO and Boli, J (1987) The political construction of mass schooling: European origins and worldwide institutionalisation. *Sociology of Education*, 60: 2–17.

Rattansi, A (1992) Changing the subject? Racism, culture and education, in Donald, J and Rattansi, A (eds) *Race, culture and difference*. London: Sage.

Reagan, T (2008) *Non-western educational traditions: indigenous approaches to educational thought and practice*, 3rd edition. Lawrence Erlbaum: New Jersey.

Reay, D (2004) 'It's all becoming a habitus': beyond the habitual use of habitus in educational research. *British Journal of Sociology of Education*, 25 (4): 431–44.

Reay, D and Wiliam, D (1999) 'I'll be a nothing': structure, agency and the construction of identity through assessment. *British Educational Research Journal*, 25 (3): 343–54.

Redhead, S (ed) (1993) *Rave off: politics and deviance in contemporary youth culture (popular cultural studies).* Farnham: Ashgate.

Rex, J (1989) Equality of opportunity, multiculturalism, anti-racism and 'education for All' in Verma, G (ed) *Education for all: a landmark in pluralism*. London: Routledge.

Rhodes, R (1997). *Understanding governance: policy networks, governance and accountability*. Buckingham: Open University Press.

Richardson, R (2006) To BME or not to BME? Questions, notes and thoughts about language, again. [online] Insted Inservice Training and Development **www.insted.co.uk/bme-article.pdf** (accessed 3 March 2009).

Richardson, R and Miles, B (2003) *Equality stories: recognition, respect and raising achievement.* Stoke on Trent: Trentham.

Richardson, R and Wood, A (2000) *Inclusive schools, inclusive society.* Stoke on Trent: Trentham Books.

Riding, R and Rayner, S (1998) *Cognitive styles and learning strategies: understanding style differences in learning and behaviour.* London: Fulton.

Rogoff, B, Mistry, J, Goencue, A and Mosier, K (1993) *Guided participation in cultural activity by toddlers and caregivers* (Monographs of the Society for Research in Child Development). Chicago: University of Chicago Press.

Rosaldo, R (1989) *Culture and truth: the remaking of social analysis.* Boston: Beacon Press.

Rosamund, B (2002) Learning about politics, in Axford, B, Browning, GK, Huggins, R, Rosamond, B and Turner, J *Politics: an introduction.* London: Routledge.

Rose, J (2008) *The independent review of the primary curriculum: interim report.* London: Department of Schools, Children and Families.

Rosenthal, R and Jacobsen, L (2003) *Pygmalion in the classroom: teacher expectation and pupils' intellectual development,* new edition. Carmarthen: Crown House Publishing.

Royal Society for the Encouragement of Arts, Manufactures and Commerce (RSA) (1999) *Opening minds: education for the 21st century.* London: Royal Society for the Encouragement of Arts, Manufactures and Commerce (RSA). **www.thersa.org/projects/education/opening-minds/start-using-opening-minds-publications-and-resources** (accessed 3 March 2009).

Rudduck, J and Fielding, M (2006) Student voice and the perils of popularity. *Educational Review,* 58 (2): 219–31.

Russell, R and Tyler, M (2002) Thank heaven for little girls: 'girl heaven' and the commercial context of feminine childhood'. *Sociology,* 37 (3): 619–37.

Sapir, E (1921) *Language: an introduction to the study of speech.* New York: Harcourt, Brace and Company.

Scanlon, L (2008) How real is reel? Teachers on screen and in the classroom. *Australian Review of Public Affairs,* September 2008. **www.australianreview.net/digest/2008/09/scanlon.html** (accessed 18 February 2009).

Schech, S and Haggis, J (2000) *Culture and development: a critical introduction.* Oxford: Blackwell.

Schofield, JW (1995) *Computers and classroom culture.* Cambridge: Cambridge University Press.

Schwartz, P (2001). *Problem-based learning: case studies, experience and practice.* London: Kogan Page.

Select Committee on Race Relations and Immigration (1969) *The problems of coloured school-leavers* (Parliamentary Papers Reports). London: HMSO.

Sharp, J, Bowjer, R and Byrne, J (2008) VAK or VAK-uous? Towards the trivialisation of learning and the death of scholarship. *Research Papers in Education,* 23 (3): 293–314.

Shirazi, R (2007) Schooling in Afghanistan, in Gupta A (ed) *Going to school in South Asia.* Westport: Greenwood Press.

Smith, M (2008) Howard Gardner and multiple intelligences. *The Encyclopaedia of Informal Education,* **www.infed.org/thinkers/gardner.htm** (accessed 23 February 2009).

Sontag, S (1996) *Thirty years later . . .* **www.threepennyreview.com/samples/sontag_su96.html** (accessed 23 February 2009).

Spring, JH (2000) *The universal right to education: justification, definition and guidelines.* New Jersey: Lawrence Erlbaum.

Stein, S (2004) *The culture of education policy*. New York: Teachers College Press.

Stephens, P, Leach, A, Jones, H and Taggart, L (1998) *Think sociology*. Cheltenham: Nelson.

Storry, M and Childs, P (2002) *British cultural identities*. London: Routledge.

Stott, T (2001) Quangos: are they unloved and misunderstood?, in Robins, L and Jones, J (eds) *Debates in British politics today*. Manchester: Manchester University Press.

Stronach, I and Piper H (2008) Can liberal education make a comeback? The case of 'relational touch' at Summerhill School. *American Educational Research Journal*, 45 (1): 6–37.

Swann Report (1985) *Education for all: report of the Committee of Enquiry into the Education of Children from Ethnic Minority Groups*. Cmnd 9453. London: HMSO.

Taylor, C (1994) The politics of recognition, in Gutmann, A (ed) *Multiculturalism: examining the politics of recognition*. Princeton: Princeton University Press.

Taylor, S, Rizvi, R, Lingard, B and Henry, M (1997) *Educational policy and the politics of change*. London: Routledge.

Tomlinson, S (2005) *Education in a post-welfare society*. Maidenhead: Open University Press.

Tomlinson, S (1983) *Ethnic minorities in British schools: a review of the literature 1960–1982*. London: Heinemann.

TRLP (2007) *Principles into practice: a teacher's guide to research evidence on teaching and learning*. Teaching and Learning Research Programme.

Troyna, B and Williams, J (1985) *Racism, education, and the state: the racialisation of education policy*. London: Routledge.

Troyna, B and Hatcher, R (1992) *Racism in children's lives: a study of mainly-white primary schools*. London: Routledge.

Tutt, R (2006) Reconciling the irreconcilable: coping with contradictory agendas' *Forum*, 48 (2): 209–16.

Vaughan, M (2006) *Summerhill and AS Neill*. Maidenhead: Open University Press.

Wain, K (2006) Contingency, education, and the need for reassurance. *Studies in Philosophy and Education*, 25 (1/2): 37–45.

Walford, G (2004) Education, in Pickering, WSF (ed) *Durkheim today*. New York: Berghan Books.

Wardekker, W (2001) Schools and moral education: conformism or autonomy? *Journal of Philosophy of Education*, 35 (1): 101–14.

Weber, E (1976) *Peasants into Frenchmen: the modernization of rural France, 1880–1914*. Stanford: Stanford University Press.

Wessels, T (2006). *The myth of progress: toward a sustainable future*. Burlington: University of Vermont Press.

Wetz, J (2008) The children left behind. *Dispatches*, Channel 4 (11 February 2008).

Whelan, R (ed) (2007) *The corruption of the curriculum*. London: Civitas and Cromwell Press.

Williams, F (2004) What matters is who works: why every child matters to New Labour. Commentary on the DfES Green Paper *Every Child Matters*. *Critical Social Policy*, 24 (3): 406–27.

Williams, R (1983) *Keywords: a vocabulary of culture and society*. New York: Oxford University Press US.

Willis, P (1977) *Learning to Labour*. Farnborough: Saxon House.

Wright, R (2006) *A short history of progress*. Edinburgh: Canongate Books.

Wood, D (1996) *Post-intellectualism and the decline of democracy: the failure of reason and responsibility in the twentieth century*. Westport: Greenwood Press.

Wood, D (1997) *How children think and learn: the social contexts of cognitive development*, 2nd edition. Oxford: Wiley-Blackwell.

Woods, P, Ashley, M and Woods, G (2005) *Steiner schools in England*. London: DFES.

Woolfolk, A, Hughes, M and Walkup V (2008) *Psychology in education*. Harlow: Pearson Education.

Wrigley, T (2006) *Another school is possible*. London: Bookmarks.

Index